BOOK

OF

HUNTING SONGS

AND

SPORT.

COLLECTED BY

MRS. CHAWORTH MUSTERS,

AND DEDICATED TO

THE RIGHT HON. EARL FERRERS,

M.F.H.

1885.

CONTENTS.

"WE were much pleased lately with the snuggery of a great ex-huntsman, where we turned in for a couple of hours to chat of old times. Among the prints was a very characteristic one of old Meynell, sitting in his study-chair and pigtail, and giving orders to Jack Raven, who stands with a comfortable little corporation at the door. Jack appears in the well-known Billesdon picture on Loadstone, opening the gate with his whip; but the old horse wants no more, and resolutely puts his foot in the gate, while Mr. Lorraine Smith is wading with his coat, like an old woman's petticoats, in his hand. The drawing is bad, but the song which illustrates it is so scarce, and those few who possess it seem to have it only in MS., that we reprint it here, simply premising that there are one or two names of which there may be a different reading."

A HUNTING SONG.

TUNE—"DERBY DOWN."

Was there ever such work? as our leaders oft say;
Was there ever yet seen such a glorious day?
Not Meynell himself, the king of all men,
Ever saw such a chase, or will see such again.

Derry Down.

Billesdon Coplow 's the place where the contest began,
And away from the covert bold Reynard soon ran:
Two hours and a quarter, I think, was the time—
It was beautifully great, nay indeed 'twas sublime.
                              Derry Down.

At Skeffington earths the villain did try,
Then, making all speed, to Tilton Wood did he fly:
By Skeffington Town he soon after came back,
And at Tugby was near being caught by the pack.
                              Derry Down.

Then passing by Stretton to Wigstone he went,
And at Ailstone we thought that the rogue must be spent;
But for crossing the river he found a good place,
And, changing at Enderby, finished the chase.
                              Derry Down.

Scotch, Welsh, Irish, and English, together set out,
And each thought his horse than his neighbour's more stout.
You must judge by the nags which were in at the end
Which riders to judge and which to commend.
                              Derry Down.

Lorraine and Lord Maynard were there, and could tell
Who in justice's scale held the balance so well,
As very good judges and justices too,
The state of each horse, and what each man could do.
                              Derry Down.

But if anyone thinks he is grieved in the song,
And fancies his case stated legally wrong,
To Enderby Hall let him go and complain,
But he won't mend his cause if he meets with Lorraine.
                              Derry Down.

Germaine, the most gallant, was first at the river;
Like a spaniel dashed in—how he made our hearts quiver!
And as Albion, as bold, he gave Mellon a pull,
And beat thro' the stream like Europa's famed bull.
Derry Down.

Jack Musters, delighted at this bright example,
Close on the dun's heels in the water did trample.
He held by the tail, and got safe to the bank,
Though the water ran over the grey horse's flank.
Derry Down.

Cox stood on the brink, and would fain have gone arter,
But the hydrophobia made him turn at the water;
So he scrambled away as fast as he could,
And got up with the hounds at Enderby Wood.
Derry Down.

We have not much to say of Morpath and Shelley,
They at Skeffington stopped, I suppose, for a jelly.
It is true they ride hard, and are said to be keen,
But yet in this run they never were seen.
Derry Down.

What came of Bob Grosvenor no poet can tell;
Not long with the pack did the gay bishop dwell;
He met brother South, and 'twas said by the people,
That the parsons were perched up on Skeffington steeple.
Derry Down.

There they sat quite contented, like parson and clerk,
And talked over things until very near dark,
Till the bishop began to take fright at the weather,
And their nags being fresh they reached Melton together.
Derry Down.

As 'twas late in the day the gallant Lord Craven,
Finding matters grow serious, kept his eye on Jack Raven ;
But the old Raven croaked when his horse was near done,
So he changed with Ben Rowland and finished the run.
Derry Down.

In this state of distress my Lord Maddock saw,
Who just in his nag had discovered a flaw ;
Together they joined, and took leave of the pack ;
Maddock trudged home, but the peer got a hack.
Derry Down.

Of Bobby Montgomery, Messrs. Waddle and Cuff,
As they say they can ride, I would fain say enough :
Their riding displayed a spread eagle complete,
And to those who were near must have proved a great
    treat.   Derry Down.

Charles Meynell got in, but how he got there
No sportsman could tell, for he made them all stare.
We heard that the waggon had just passed the road—
Why did not the waggoner stop with his load ?
Derry Down.

Of Joey Pantigious, 'tis said in a burst
He finds it quite easy being second or first.
We'd a chase on the pike, and he drove in his gig ;
I then bet two to one on the little Pound Pig.
Derry Down.

Of a mighty great king, how it lowered his pride
To be walking on foot when his subjects did ride ;
Though they passed by in numbers to no one he spoke,
But like Charley the Second got up in the oak.
Derry Down.

Tho' late in the song, yet perish the thought
That our gallant friend Villiers should e'er be forgot;
Some disaster, I fancy, his lordship befell,
As he did not get in, tho' he rides very well.
Derry Down.

Lord Charles rode on Marquis, so famed for his blood,
And shared in all dangers except in the flood.
Charles Ellis came up, but he got a fresh horse,
And we saw by the change that he was not the worse.
Derry Down.

By the bye, I forgot to name Lawley of Quorn,
Tho' forward at first lamed his horse with a thorn;
And losing a shoe is sometimes the reason
Why a gentleman's beat at the end of the season.
Derry Down.

Tom Smith in the contest maintained a good place,
And tho' not first, at last made a famous good race.
I'm sure he'd no cause for his horse to abuse,
And I wish he'd persuade him to keep on his shoes.
Derry Down.

Mr. Saville and Nat dropped in at the end—
Which the best of the nags I cannot contend;
For tho' they breathe high they are still full of fire,
For he says they're so stout that they never do tire.
Derry Down.

I think now I've bored you enough with the chase,
And like Meynell's hounds I have run a good race;
Then a bumper, my boys, to Meynell we'll fill,
And to those that ride hard may they never stand still.
Derry Down.

Written by MR. BETHELL COX, from the
Sporting Magazine, 1856.

For notes to most of the heroes of this poem, see "Billesdon Coplow."

THE old Hurworth foxhounds met at Croft Bridge this morning, under the mastership of Lord Castlereagh, who was prevented being present in consequence of a death in the family.

Drew the Willow Garths and the Skerne Banks up to Blackwell Hall, when a beautiful chesnut coloured fox broke away from under the old hollies and laurels in front of the hall. The fox then crossed the Great North Road, near what used to be the Angel Inn, and continued along the banks of the river Skerne till he came opposite Black Banks earths, when he crossed over, the horsemen having to go round to a bridge near Croft. He then ran past Round Hill and Hurworth Moor Farms, leaving Fighting Cocks covert to the right, crossing the Darlington and Stockton railway, near an old drain, in which many a good fox has taken refuge in former runs. And here George Dodds, the huntsman, showed the greatest energy in getting the hounds stopped, in consequence of a long mineral train running up the line, the driver taking no notice of signs to slacken. However, no harm was done, and the hounds picked the scent up quickly on the other side of the railway, and away to Little Burdon, where he was viewed in a field adjoining the earths. On he went to Great Burdon, crossed the Skerne to Wimbush, leaving Barmpton to the right; he then re-crossed the Skerne, and, after running along the banks, crossed it again near Little Ketton, where he was viewed again on the Barmpton side into a small plantation, some of the field having to go round to a bridge near Ketton Hall, others having got over the Skerne at Barmpton. However, we all got together again near Newton Ketton. Hounds at check, in consequence of coming across some greyhounds coursing here. They picked the scent up again, and on to Great Stainton with a rattle, turned towards Stellington, then to the left to Elstob Hall, and crossed the Hartlepool railway to Bog Hall; he then took a road for about a mile to Morden Moor, crossed in front of Sands Hall, and on to Sedgefield station, where he crossed the railway, ran for two or three fields and re-crossed the railway back to Morden, and then to Bog Hall covert; never went in, but turned again to the north, and after viewing him for a few minutes the hounds ran into him at Brechon Hill farm. Time, 3 hours and 5 minutes. From point to point, 12 miles; as the fox ran, about 22. There were five checks, the longest near Newton Ketton, and another when he turned from Stellington towards Elstob, where there is a fox earth, but he never went near it. In at the finish were a friend of Lord Castlereagh's on a chesnut horse, W. G. Elliot, M.P., T. Wilkinson, R. L. Ward, C. Backhouse, A. Park, J. W. Smith, J. Brown, George Dodds the huntsman, a whip, and a servant.

Written by Rev. J. W. Smith,
Rector of Dinsdale.

"SENDE HYM ALONG;

OR,

Ye counsayle of olde Robert to Mayster Henrie, ye sonne to Squyer Nymrood."

"Come, tell me, old Robert—you can if you will—
How to go to the fore with the best of the throng;
I can sit on Bay Jerry, don't care for a spill,
And I just want to know how to send him along.

"Aye, aye, Mayster Harrie, I'll tell you with glee—
  For I'm right glad to see to th' old stock you belong;
So now for a moment just listen to me,
  And you sha'nt be the last as you send him along.

"Be in time—then drop down to the covert's lee side;
  Throw away your cigar, leave the jest and the song;
Creep in and keep quiet in some likely ride;
  Sit still—but be ready to send him along.

"Watch closely the hounds as they carefully draw—
  Mark the note of the true one that now throws his
      tongue;
Ears attend for the holloa—'away, gone away!'—
  Then down like a lightning flash send him along.

"He's away, he's away, and you're well away, too;
  You've got a good start, and there's nothing gone wrong;
The pack's all before you, all mad for a view—
  Up, up in your stirrups, and send him along.

"You're well over some big 'uns, and in the first flight;
  Never heed those that follow, pell mell and ding dong;
Never look to the left, never look to the right,
  But keep your eyes for'ard and send him along.

"The country gets closer, the brooks deep and wide,
  And some timber it looks most uncomfortably strong;
But the low viewing nag will take each in his stride
  As you sit down upon him and send him along.

"Near an hour you've been at him, the pace 'gins to tell,
  And tails they are shaking like tails in Hong Kong;
So look to your *hand*, and your head, too, as well,
  As you sit close and nurse him, yet send him along.

" He's now sinking fast—they are close at his brush—
  ' Whoo-oop!' they have got him; one crack from your
     thong,
Then jump off—get away from the wrangling rush,
  And thank Robert, who taught you to send him along."

          Written by the late REV. H. O. COXE,
                Librarian of the Bodleian.

QUORN HOUNDS, 1867.

TUNE—" WHO CAN TELL."

When will the *Marquis come? Who can tell?
Half-past twelve or half-past one? Who can tell?
Is he sober, is he drunk? Nipping like Myn heer von
    Dunk?
Will he ride or will he funk? Who can tell?

Shall we have to wait again? Who can tell?
In the wind and in the rain? Who can tell?
While the Marquis, snug and warm, in the hall where
    toadies swarm,
Leaves us to the pelting storm? Who can tell?

Where'll he draw by way of luck? Who can tell?
Gartree hill, or Bradgate Park? Who can tell?
Sport regarding as a jest, which will suit his fancy best—
North or south, or east or west? Who can tell?

---

* Harry, last Marquis of Hastings, died 1868.

Where, oh where, rings Goodall's† horn? Who can tell?
Why came I with this cursed Quorn? Who can tell?
Marquis, this is not a race; Can you look us in the face,
And declare you love the chase? Who can tell?

―――

ELEGY ON THE DEATH OF HONEST BALL.

SCENE—THE CLOSE NEXT THE ROAD AT ASTON.

'Twas on a verdant pasture's side,
Thro' which the tinkling riv'lets glide,
    And sportful lambkins play;
Where ever steady faithful Ball,
Obedient to his master's call,
    His time had grazed away.

When lo! a huntsman's voice was heard,
His head old Ball in transport reared,
    He hailed each choral hound;
The conscious snort his pride declared,
In ev'ry neigh his joy appeared—
    He spurned the trembling ground.

Of fond ideas what a train,
Of blissful pleasures what a chain,
    Then sprung into his heart!
All rapture will abound, says he,
To my good master and to me,
    That hunting can impart.

† Mr. Tailby's huntsman.

He mused, and musing called to mind
Each end-way chase with stag and hind,*
    And eke with wily fox.
Reflection echoed back the tale †
Of every hill and every dale,
    Of woods, and crags, and rocks.

Still had he mus'd, but cross his thought,
With worth intrinsically wrought,
    Stept forth a Mundy's name!
Till now Ball never knew the laws,
Nor the criterion, nor the cause
    Of modern hunter's fame.

He starts, displeas'd with bootless lore,
Which Burdett us'd in days of yore,
    Displeasure makes him rave!
Ye gods, says he, what time I've spent,
And never knew what hunting meant
    Till one foot's in the grave!

Again he cools; the gods implores,
That e'er he reach the Stygian shores
    One good day's sport be given.
He vows a day to Ticknall gorse
Will make him happier than the horse
    Which Mah'mett rode to heaven.

---

*Alluding to divers chases, in which Ball attended Mr. Shuttleworth's deer hounds.

† Alluding to a famous chase with Sir Robert's old foxhounds from Gorsty Leas quite away to Anchor-Church Rocks.

He spoke, when, bursting from a cloud,
A phantom in a silver shroud
    Forewarned him of his end.
It cried out, ' Ball, thou'rt quite undone,
And, as thy loving master's gone,
    A fav'rite has no friend.'

Ah! presage sad, 'twas but too true—
For see, the ruthless Jack's in view—
    Behold his bloody knife!
The fatal sisters gave the word,
Which Jack observ'd with fell accord,
    And clos'd the Book of Life.

Ungrateful man! is this the need
That's due to each old gen'rous steed
    For ev'ry kind relief?
Was it for this that heaven gave
Each brute to thee to be thy slave
    When thou'rt of brutes the chief.†

---

† I owe this curious old poem to the kindness of Mr. Rolleston, of Watnall, who found it among some family papers. The individuals mentioned in it I take to have been SIR ROBERT BURDETT, of Foremark, who died in 1797; FRANCIS NOEL CLARKE MUNDY, ESQ., of Markeaton, who married Sir Robert's daughter, Elizabeth, and kept a pack of hounds in Derbyshire within the memory of persons still living; and JAMES SHUTTLEWORTH, ESQ., of Gawthorp, M. P., who married Mary, the daughter and heiress of Robert Holden, Esq., of Aston, the scene of the song. I should imagine "honest Ball" to have been the property of the Rev. John Rolleston, who was for forty years Rector of Aston, and married Dorothy, the youngest daughter of Sir Robert Burdett, and died 1770.

THE FORSTEN HUNT.

AN IMITATION OR PARODY OF AN IRISH HUNTING SONG,
ADAPTED AT FORSTEN, IN THE YEAR 1761.

Hark, hark, jolly sportsmen, awhile to my tale,
To pay your attention I'm sure you can't fail;
'Tis of dogs, and of horses, and lads who ne'er tire
O'er downs or o'er heaths, thro' furze, brakes, or mire.
A pack of such hounds, and a set of such men,
'Tis shrewd chance if ever you hear of again.
Had Nimrod, that mightiest of hunters, been there,
Egad! he'd have shook like an aspen for fear.

In seventeen hundred and sixty one,
The month of December was scarcely begun;
At eight in the morning by most of the clocks
We set out from Forsten in search of a fox.
Jack Trenchard and Simnes, that parson in grey,
And Furber, the farmer, were with us that day,
*Jack Fane and †Ned Phelips, those hunters so stout,
Blair, Jones, and Tom Meggs, and so we set out.

We cast off our hounds for an hour or more,
When Piper set up a most tuneable roar.
"Hark to Piper," cries Scott; the rest were not slack,
For Piper's no babbler esteemed by the pack.
Old Miller and Polly came merrily in,
And all the hounds joined in the musical din;
Had Diana been there she'd been pleased to the life,
And one of the lads got a goddess for wife.

---

* Jack Fane, afterwards 9th Earl of Westmoreland.
+ Ned Phelips.—Edward Phelips, Esq., of Montacute.

Ten minutes past ten was the time of the day
When Reynard unkennelled, and this was the way:
From Grange to Mount Silver and Clenger he past,
Thro' Hawkham and Hackham to Kingrose at last;
O'er the hill to Fair Mile and Puddle's smooth down—
In Wootton's strong brake the caytiff did run;
The turnpike he crossed, leapt Lord Ilchester's wall,
And seemed to say, "Little I value you all."

Then close by Will Pitt's to Gallam he runs,
Blair, Jones, and Tom Meggs kept leading by turns;
The earths were all open, yet he was so stout,
Tho' he might have got in, yet he chose to keep out.
To Elsington wood like a bullet he flew—
At Tinkleton parish we had him in view;
To Frampton's bog next, o'er heaths wild and dreary,
Where Meggs and the parson and Trenchard grew weary.

Then away to the cliffs like an arrow he past,
And came near the Castle of Lulworth at last,
Where he valiantly plunged himself into the sea,
And said in his heart, "Who dares follow me?"
But soon to his cost he perceived that no bounds
Could stop the pursuit of the staunch mettled hounds.
His policy here did not serve him a rush—
Five couple of tartars were close at his brush.

To recover the shore again was his drift,
But, e'er he could get to the top of the clift,
He found both of strength and of cunning a lack—
Killed, worried, and torn by the rest of the pack.
At his death there were present the lads whom I've sung,
Save poor Jacky Trenchard, whom Badger had flung,
And thus we concluded this delicate chase,
Which lasted three hours and ten minutes' space.

At eve we returned home to Forsten again.
Where dwells hospitality, truth, and Jack Fane.
We talked o'er the chase, and we toasted the health
Of the man who ne'er varies for places or wealth.
"Charles Blair* baulked a leap," says Phelips; "'twas
   odd;"
"'Twas shameful," cried Jones, "by the great living God."
Says Meggs, "I hallooed, get on, tho' you fall,
Or I'll leap over you, your blind stone horse and all."

To the drawing room next, for Augusta,† the fair,
And Woodford, the merriest of damsels, were there:
Ned Phelips' sister, Maria, his wife,
And the girl Ben Simnes had just taken for life.
No scandal or folly their converse dispense,
But wit with good humour, and mirth with good sense.
As Pallas and Dian the hunters befriend,
The muses and graces these ladies attend.

Our evening, devoted to freedom and sport,
All party affairs we consigned to the court.
The ladies, the fairest Britannia can boast,
Were each in their turn proclaimed as a toast;
And thus we concluded the day and the night
In jollity, sport, and in social delight.
And as Phœbus befriended our earlier roam,
So Luna took care to conduct us safe home. ‡

---

* Charles Blair afterwards married Lady Mary Fane, and, with "Jones,"
was guardian to John, 10th Earl of Westmoreland.

† Mrs. John Fane, daughter of Lord Albemarle Bertie.

‡ Forsten, "where dwelt hospitality, truth, and Jack Fane," is three
miles north of Dorchester. From Grange Wood, where they "unkennelled"
their fox, to Lulworth Shore, where they killed him, is twenty and a half miles,
as the crow flies.

DEAR MRS. MUSTERS,

I am no hand at writing a run, but can give you the following particulars of the one you mention. The date was Monday, January 28th, 1878. The Blankney hounds met at the 7th milestone, Newark road. We found directly in Tunman's Wood, and came away over the Newark and Lincoln road, ran past Haddington to Hykeham plantation, which we left a field to the left, and on past South Hykeham, over the line close to Waddington station, and up the hill into Waddington village. Here all the rest of the field got some wrong information, and lost the hounds, and I had them all to myself over the heath past Giles' Gorse to Branston, where we had a check, and Harry Dawkins, the huntsman, and the first whip, who had ridden by my tracks over the heath, caught me up. We went straight on through the Park at Long Hills, past the end of Potterhanworth wood; but our fox was headed a field off the wood, and turned to his left and got to ground in a rabbit hole in a small plantation, called Curtis', about a mile further on. Only Harry Dawkins, the first whip, and myself, were with the hounds when they stopt. Mr. Cooke, a farmer from Scarle, came up afterwards, and we never saw anybody else. It is an eleven mile point, and was all down wind, and was the straightest run I ever saw; none of it very fast, but a good holding pace. The fox never touched a covert from find to finish.

EDWARD H. NEVILE.

THE 19TH JANUARY, 1793.

MR. MEYNELL's hounds met at Alsop's house (near Wymeswold), and found in the old cover; went away by Mr. Gooden's cover to Hell Hole, over part of Gotham Moor, over Leak Hills and Field, by Wysall, Keyworth, Kinoulton, Hickling, by Nether Broughton, Holwell, Scalford, to Goadby Park, and killed.

The hounds ran very hard for two hours and a half, all the horses being tired except Mr. Deverill's grey mare, Gaylass.

THE 22ND OF MARCH, 1793.

MR. MEYNELL's hounds met at Whitehorse Wood. Found in Bardon Hill; came away over the Rocks, Gracedieu Park, Oakley Wood, Donington Park, and run to ground at Gorsty Leas. (This is a ten mile point, and most unusual line.)

From the diary of J. JONES, Mr. Meynell's whipper-in.

WEDNESDAY, FEBRUARY 9TH, 1881.

The snow, and frost, and fog were gone,
And " cheerly smiled the morn;"
And many a sportsman's heart beat high
To hear the well-known horn.

To the Magna Charta, Lowdham,
 From far and near they come;
Some kindred souls from Derbyshire—
 Across the river, some.

Then, as the phalanx moved along
 The road to Bleasby Gorse,
With a watchful eye I scanned them,
 Ev'ry man and ev'ry horse.

Like a lovely chequered ribbon
 The little pack advance;
Fresh as paint, and bright as satin,
 They long to lead the dance.

First comes Rolleston (1) upon Rocket,
 With a thoughtful huntsman's air;
Taking counsel with George Shepherd, (2)
 Neat and jaunty as his mare.

Next, noblemen in scarlet coats,
 And gentlemen in black,
And ladies fair, and riders rare,
 And Lielly (3) on a hack.

But Bleasby holds no customer—
 They cheer and "haicks" in vain,
While we sit cooling visibly,
 Predicting it will rain.

---

1. Lancelot Rolleston, Esq., master and huntsman of the South ‹
 hounds from 1876 to 1882.

2. George (really German) Shepherd, first whip and kennel hunt
to Mr. Musters, Mr. Rolleston, and Lord Harrington successively
deservedly respected by all in the South Notts. country.

3. John Liell Francklin, Esq., of Gonalston, late M. F. H.

Halloughton Wood—"but shall we find here ?"
  Some say doubtfully and low.
Hark ! that piercing scream is George's—
  Now then, Talent, you may go.

How they race to get a start—see,
  Straight *at* the fox they ride !
And thrust and sputter in the ploughs
  That skirt the Dumble side.

Up to Bleasby, out towards Morton,
  Then round through Southwell parks,
Where o'er a gate Lord Petersham (4)
  Had one of his old larks.

And Fillingham, (5) that crafty man,
  Here jumped a fence with glee ;
And Howett (6) still, thro' good and ill,
  Is riding wild and free.

The doughty Daft (7) is here o'erthrown,
  Not by Australian ball ;
But always quick on greensward,
  Hurries Peter to a fall.

The master's down and up again,
  And Rocket's pulling still ;
And Henry Smith (8) is close behind,
  Sinking the Halam Hill.

---

4. The present Earl of Harrington, born 1844. Now hunting the South
Notts. country, 1883.
  5. George Fillingham, Esq., of Syerston, a well-known and thorough
sportsman.
  6. Mr. Robert Howett, of Woodborough, a great promoter of hunting.
  7. Mr. Daft, of Radcliffe, the celebrated cricketer.
  8. Henry Smith, Junr., of the Grove, Cropwell Butler, a keen and
hereditary sportsman.

But when the hounds swing left again,
  And past the Ash-Holts race,
And circle right round Halloughton Wood,
  What tells at last is pace.

For oh! that eager morning field,
  So gallant and so gay,
Now hounds seem running for their fox,
  Behold their sad array :

They scarce can trot, and far less jump—
  The prudent now go home,
Never thinking that the best fun
  Is only yet to come.

But who is here so full of cheer—
  A fresh horse full of ride?
Squire Sherbrooke, (9) who has nicked them,
  Running the Dumble side.

For an hour and forty minutes
  They have hunted through the plough—
See, the fox lies down before them!
  They surely have him now.

Not a bit; for over Halam,
  On tow'rds Edingley they stream;
Onward, onward over Hexgrave—
  'Tis a run we sometimes dream.

Now they're checking, we thank goodness,
  As we reach the welcome sand;
Gallant Rolt (10) has had a crumpler;
  Oxton's Squire embraced the land.

---

9. Henry Sherbrooke, Esq., of Oxton, who had been attending the
Rufford Hunt meeting at Ollerton; and on his return, coming out to look for
the hounds, by the greatest good luck fell in with them at this point.
  10. Captain Rolt, a writer in the sporting papers.

They've hit it off through Inkersall,
   Culloden's looming near;
Sporting Skelton, (11) thrusting Meeson,
   Look grave when they get here.

Pittance Park they now are skirting,
   Where our fox finds many a friend;
Like the Coplow run of history,
   Without a kill we end.

Two of Thoresby's worthy scions, (12)
   Two of Derby's sportsmen true, (13)
One descendant (14) of Jack Musters
   Saw this fine run fairly through.

Francklin, Charlton, (15) Mills, (16) and Hibbert, (17)
   Who besides must others say,
For I long had been defeated
   On my little mare so gay.

Eleven miles from point to point,
   Full thirty all they ran;
Let us drink their healths this evening—
   Fox and hound, and horse, and man. (18)

                 L. C. MUSTERS.

---

11. Mr. Skelton, the steeplechase rider, and Mr. Meeson, a friend of Mr. Howett.
12. Lord Newark and his brother, Hon. Henry Pierrepont, who died the following year.
13. Lord Petersham and Mr. Palmer, of Stanton.
14. Miss Catherine Chaworth Musters.
15. Nicolas Charlton, Esq., of Chilwell.
16. Mr. Mills, of Burton Joyce.
17. Mr. Hibbert, of Nottingham.
18. From Bleasby Gorse, the furthest point to the south, to Culloden plantation, near Rufford, eleven miles.

REMINISCENCES OF THE SHOWS OF FOXHOUNDS AT OSBERTON,

ABOUT 1825.

Oh Charley,* from Betley, how dare you appear
With your Staffordshire turnspits in Nottinghamshire,
And before the fine judgment of Lambton to bring
A son of your Joker—some poor wretched thing—
Against Pipers and Nestors to bear off a prize.
Oh Charley ! hold hard, lest a thought should arise,
That hunting in coal pits has blinded your eyes.
The praises of Joker you've trumpeted forth
O'er London's grand city and far thro' the north,
Till you've cheated yourself into thinking, alas !
That a trumpet of silver you'd gain for your brass ;
Or if broadcloth has tempted you hither to come,
How dismal the prospect next winter at home :
No saddle to shield you, no cloth will you win,
And Joker will prove a bad jest for your skin.

E. HODSON.

This was a letter from Mr. Hodson to Mr. Wicksted before Mr. Foljambe's hound show, at which Mr. Wicksted's hound, Joker, took the prize of a horn for the master and a saddle and broadcloth for coats for the men.

---

* Charles Wicksted, Esq., of Betley, born 1796 ; also mentioned in "The Woore Country," which he hunted. He afterwards kept a most beautiful pack of harriers, a few of which his son, the present George Wicksted, brought to Oxford, and with them established the Christchurch harriers. Mr. Wicksted died in 1870. His second son and namesake is the present master of the Ludlow hounds, and to him I am indebted for these amusing epistles.

Mr. Wicksted's Reply.

Oh Nestor! to joke thus how can you begin?
Forgetting the proverb, " let those laugh who win."
Your trencher-fed puppies won't win you one prize—
Saddle, broadcloth, or trumpet, to gladden your eyes.
Ere old Wells's coat shall be shorn of its skirts
Both you and Will Danby shall work in your shirts;
For no Holderness tailor shall measure a stitch
Of the broadcloth that's won by Holderness bitch.
You must use your old saddles and break your old reins
With pulling old screws thro' the Holderness drains.
Of the silver-tongued trumpet depend on't no hound
On the far side of Humber will e'er hear a sound.
So from joking forbear—it will prove a wrong cast—
For you're sure to be beat by a Joker at last.

THE HURWORTH FOX CHASE:

A BALLAD, WRITTEN ON THE OCCASION OF A MOST REMARKABLE RUN WITH MR. CHARLES TURNER'S HOUNDS ON THE 1ST DAY OF SEPT., 1775.

Attend, jolly sportsmen, I'll sing you a song,
Which cannot fail pleasing the old and the young.
I'll sing of a famous old fox and his wiles,
And lead you a dance of at least fifty miles.
I'll tell you a tale of such men and such hounds,
With what courage they bound o'er all sorts of grounds;
How dogs vie with dogs, and how men with men strive—
Old Draper may rue that he was not alive.

At Hurworth, fam'd village, as soon as 'twas light,
We feasted our eyes with a ravishing sight:
Each sportsman had pleasure and health in his face,
And horses and hounds were all ripe for the chase.
But first, the commander-in-chief I should name,
The lord of Kirkleatham, of right honest fame,
A friend to good men, but profess'dly a foe
To villains of four legs as well as of two.
We had not tried long before Rafter gave mouth—
Esteemed by the pack as the standard of truth.
They quickly fly to him, and instant declare
That Rafter was right, for a fox had been there;
And, trust me, he proved a notorious blade.
His name was Old Cæsar, and plunder his trade:
His namesake, in all the great battles he won,
Spilled less blood by gallons than this rogue had done.
Unken'lling at Eyreholme, he first tried a round
In which he might run about four miles of ground.
Then back to the earths, but the stopper took care
To baulk him from making his quarters good there.
Disdaining such treatment he flourished his brush,
And seemed to say, "Sportsmen, I care not a rush;
I'll give you such proofs of my stoutness and speed
That Nimrod himself would have honoured the breed."
By Smeaton and Hornby he next took his way,
Resolved to make this a remarkable day;
Then wheeled to the left for the banks of the Tees,
But there he could meet neither safety nor ease.
Now finding with what sort of hounds he'd to deal,
And that his pursuers were true men of steel,
He pushed to gain shelter in Craythorne Wood,
The hounds at his brush all eager for blood.
The field all alive, now we smoaked him along,
So joyous the music, each note was a song—
All round us was melody, spirit, and joy.

Next passing by Marten and Ormesby Hall,
He seemed to say, "Little I value you all."
For many a stout horse was now dropping his speed,
And to see them tail off was diverting indeed.
Now found to be thought no contemptible fox,
He dared us to follow up mountains and rocks:
But th' ascent was so steep and so painfully won,
That few gained the Eston Hall before he was gone.
To Kirkleatham Park he nexts points his career,
Hard pressed by the owner to spend his life there;
Assuring him he and his guests would not fail
All possible honour to render his tail.
But Turner being now left alone on the field,
And finding Old Cæsar unwilling to yield,
At Kilton thought proper to finish the strife,
So called off the dogs to give Cæsar his life.
But Blue Bell and Bonny Lass would have a meal—
Whose hearts are of oak, and whose loins are of steel—
So followed him up to his friends of the mill,
Where triumphant they seized him and feasted their fill.
Then, just like attraction 'twixt needle and pole,
All center'd that evening in Kirkleatham Hall,
Where the bottle of red and the fox-hunting bowl
Not only refreshed but exalted the soul.
Then may the kind host long continue to grace
His country, his mansion, and also the chase;
And, long as old Time shall be measured by clocks,
May a Turner for ever prevail o'er a fox.

By the Rev. Mr. Bramwell,
Rector of Hurworth.

THE BEDALE HOUNDS IN 1838.

Here's to the old ones of fox-hunting fame,
  Cleveland, Ralph Lampton and Harewood ;
Here's to the young ones that after them came
  Who will not say that they *are* good.

Here's to the master,(1) well skilled in the art
  To kill an old fox in all weathers ;
Here's to the riders, all ready to start,
  Brilliant in boots and in leathers.

Here's to the hounds, all vigour and bone,
  In condition excelling all others ;
Here's to old Barwick,(2) who stands quite alone
  In cheering them on thro' the covers.

Here's to the Sportsmen, I give you each name,
  Their feats and their fortunes in detail ;
North Riding heroes, all eager for fame,
  To be reaped in the country of Bedale.

On Borderer mounted see Milbank ride.
  Three hundred won't buy such a horse, sir ;
Limbs with no check to their freedom of stride,
  Wind without whistle or cough, sir.

"Tally Ho ! Toot a toot ! he is gone," says the squire—
  Let any one catch them who can, sir :
Who rides with my hounds a good horse will require,
  And himself he must be a good man, sir.

Here's to the Duke,(3) if he leads not still Leeds,
  To borrow a joke from his grace, sir ;
A nobleman true, both in word and in deeds,
  And the firmest support of the chase, sir.

---

1. Mr. Milbank, of Thorp Perrow, died 1883. 2. Mr. Milbank's first whip.
3. The 6th Duke of Leeds, of whom Lord Darlington says, "The brilliancy of the duke of Leeds's strict and assiduous preservation of the noble animal, the fox, showed forth most conspicuously to-day, and was as bright a gem as any in his grace's star, and most thankfully acknowledged by me."

Here's to the Græme,(4) who does not disdain
  In a north country province to ride, sir;
Forgetting that once, thro' the Leicestershire plain,
  Scarce a rival could live by his side, sir.

Here's to the Colonel,(5) if warm be his name,
  Both that and his heart go together;
In pleasant discourse, whilst we ride down the lane,
  Let us be in no hurry to sever.

Here's to friend George, the beau of Camphill,
  A good one, if fast be the chase, sir;
To pass him, I tell you, requires as much skill
  As Fieschi, when he won the race, sir.

Here's to the Baron of Sawley so sly,—
  Here's to his horse that is black, sir;
Forgetting that always a crow cannot fly,
  He fell o'er a fence on his back, sir,

Here's to Straubenzee, the dashing and bold,
  Taking all in his stroke like a man, sir;
And the pith of the story remains to he told—
  You can't shake him off from the "Van," sir.

Here's to the Major, the gallant and true,
  In riding to no one he'll yield, sir;
See, he brings by his side a young damsel in view,
  To beat half the men in the field, sir.

Here's to Dundas's,(6) both Thomas and John,
  They come but to make us remember
How short is their stay—for to London they're gone
  Ere the end of the month of November.

---

4. Sir Bellingham Graham.
5. Colonel Arden.
6. Sons of the first Earl of Zetland.

Here's to the young ones, whose race scarce begun,
   Young Mark, and the ensign, his brother;
They show of a stock most goodly they come,
   As they tread in the steps of their father. (7)

The gallant, the ardent, of promise so fair,
   The Beresford brothers they bring;
A word from my pen must give them their share
   Of the honours and glories I sing.

Many good ones remain—Hodson, Crompton, and Tower,
   Fox, Ward, and the young one from Norton;
But to mention them all is not in my power,
   So, surely it cannot be thought on.

And here's to the squire of Thirsk, Jack Bell, (8)
   Who supports both the chase and the turf, sir;
He will not, unless he likes it, go well,
   Tho' the hounds may run ever so fast, sir.

Here's a bumper to Milbank, the source of our sport—
   A bumper to him and his hounds, sir;
Brim-full it shall be of the finest old port,
   Where health and good humour abound, sir.

And may we all flourish till green our old age is,
   Such fun and such sport to pursue, sir;
And your "lame" humble poet to be hanged now engages
   If his composition's not true, sir.

        By the REV. JOHN MONSON,
      from "Recollections of Sportsmen," &c.,
        by Colonel Van Straubenzee.

---

7. Mr. Milbank's sons.
8. Master of the Hambledon hounds.

THE PROPHET IN HIS OWN COUNTRY;

OR, DUFTY IN DERBYSHIRE.

187—.

In the days of Percy Williams, (1)
　　In the time of Scarbro's peer,(2)
Lived at Epperstone a sportsman
　　Keen of sight and quick of ear.
Looking down a grassy riding,
　　Or across his Dumbles dear,
Never could a fox evade him,
　　Or escape his ringing cheer.

Far away in Winkburn woodlands,
　　Or in Rufford's forest glade;
From the ancient gorse of Bleasby
　　To the Blidworth fir trees' shade;
Ev'ry earth and smeuse he knows them,
　　Ev'ry hole that e'er was made.
" What a whipper-in is lost there,"
　　Wond'ring at him, people said.

By and by, when Squire Musters, (3)
　　Who to sport did ever lean,
Wanted to revive the glories
　　That in South Notts. once were seen;

---

1. Captain Percy Williams, the celebrated gentleman huntsman, master of the Rufford hounds from 1841 to 1860.
2. John, 8th Earl of Scarbro', died 1856.
3. John Chaworth Musters, born 1838. Hunted the South Notts. country from 1861 to 1868, the Quorn from 1868 to 1870, and, returning to South Notts. in 1871, hunted that country till 1876, when he was obliged, through ill-health, to give up his hounds.

Saying, " Let us have some foxhounds—
  That may be which once has been."
Who so full of zeal as Dufty ? (4)
  Who so anxious ? who so keen ?

Still the same as years pass o'er him,
  Clad in sportsmanlike array;
Hunting always finds him ready
  With a scent to sail away.
Does a flooded brook need fording ?
  Dufty's here and knows the way.
Does a straight-necked fox want finding ?
  What has Dufty got to say ?

So at last we grew to think him
  Filled with wisdom more than man ;
Wily in the ways of creatures—
  Fause as any fox that ran.
One fine day our master, Rolleston, (5)
  Hunting always all he can,
Thinks to please his good friend Dufty,
  And unfolds to him this plan :—

" On next Saturday we're going
  To a country rich and rare ;
Full of covers, grass, and foxes—
  Oh ! the scents that we have there !
You shall bring your horse to Gedling—
  Place him in the train with care,
Then be wafted smooth and swiftly
  To that land beyond compare."

---

4. Thomas Dufty, of Epperstone, one of the best of sportsmen, and the hero of this poem.
5. Lancelot Rolleston, of Watnall. Hunted the South Notts. country from 1876 to 1882.

To the tempter Dufty listened.
　　When the morning came he went,
Travelled by Great Northern Railway,
　　Still on Horsley Car intent.
When he got there, quite delighted,
　　(Covers, foxes, grass, and scent,)
All he found that he'd been told off—
　　"This is what the master meant."

Later on, that winter evening,
　　Coxbench covers must be drawn.
"Dufty, you stand here to view him,
　　Close beside that black old thorn."
You, I know, won't let him slip you;
　　You're a man one need not warn."
Small this cover is, and hollow—
　　Foxes here must soon be gone.

Hark! the joyful news proclaiming!
　　Foxhounds' music fills the air;
Ev'ry heart beats loud and gaily,
　　Waiting Dufty's welcome cheer.
Strange! the silence still unbroken—
　　To that end he ran 'tis clear;
Hounds come pouring to the corner—
　　"Sir, I'm sure he's not gone here."

Can I tell this wondrous story:
　　How he passed 'neath Dufty's nose;
Ran right down the ditch below him,
　　Almost grazed his horse's toes?
Sad and scornful were the murmurs
　　From the strangers there that rose.
South Notts. men must now knock under—
　　Derbyshire o'er Dufty crows.
　　　　　　　　　　L. C. MUSTERS.

AN EXACT ACCOUNT OF THE FOX CHASE ON YE 2ND OF
DECEMBER, 1745, BY HIS GRACE THE DUKE OF
GRAFTON'S HOUNDS, AS FOLLOWS :—

UNKENNELD at half an hour past nine of the clock in
the forenoon at Ladis Carr, near the Decoy in Euston,
and from thence came away over the Heath to the Marle
Pit, through Honington and by Sapson Carr. From
thence to Bangor Bridge, came along the late Mrs.
Reade's Carr, and cross the road by Back Bridge.
Went away for Stanton Chair, over the deal, and past
Stanton earth, and then through ye corn grounds, the
back side of Hepworth common to Seacey's hole, when
we turned towards the right, and came thro' Walsham-
le-Willows; and then for Langham common down to
Stow-langtoft, and across the river between Wayley
poole and Stow bridge, and then to Packenham wood,
and from thence to ye Kiln grounds, the back side of
Thurston common. From thence to Beighton groves,
and on to Drinkston and Hesset groves, and near Moule
wood, and past Drinkston Hall; and from thence to
Rattlesden, between the great wood and the street, and
thro' Haisel grove to Wood Hall, when ye hounds were
at a check for two or three minutes, which was ye only
check during the whole chase. The huntsman took a
half cast, and hit it off, and came away across Buxhall,
Fen Street, and from thence to Norfield, and by Fox
Hill Grove, and across the Stow Market road to Day-
worth hills, and thro' old Newton and bear-gipping
wood; then away for Stow upland, and from
thence to West Creeting, over the green by Ray-
don Hall; then we turned on the right and came
down to Combs, and across the two rivers by Cook's
water mill, and across the road between Combsford and

Stow Market wind mills, and then thro' Mr. John Baylis' cheny yard to the sign of the Shepherd and Dog in one house, and killed by some hop yards, near William Wollaston's, Esq., at four of the clock in the afternoon.

N.B.—This is as Brief an account as can be given, notwithstanding there was several Rings and Turns too tedious to insert here. Ran through twenty-eight Parishes, which in whole, upon a moderate computation, is sixty miles by care.

JOHN GOODRICH.

Copied by the Duke of Grafton from an old sporting book at Euston Hall, 1860 (from A. Hamond).

Euston to Creeting is seventeen miles as the crow flies.—L. C. M.

A RUN WITH THE "WEST OF FIFE."

FEBRUARY 2ND, 1877.

Loud blows the wind around the house,
Rain dashes on the pane;
The Western Hunt bemoan their fate,
For the meet is Pitfirrane.

But, nothing daunted, on they pull
Their breeches, spurs, and boots;
And come in Red, and some in Black,
And some in other suits.

A few appear on wheels that day,
And two have come by rail;
But if I counted all who came,
'Twould make too long a tale.

The Hounds were brought before the door,
And gathered in a cluster;
Their eyes shone bright,
High waved their sterns,
Their coats all shone with lustre.

The Master in the middle sits
Upon his mare " Gazette;"
Says he, " The ground is very deep,
" But I'll be with 'em yet."

Jack Shepherd, on the kicking mare,
Is eager for the fray;
And Harry Sinclair, second whip,
Is on the snorting grey.

But time is up, so let us move,
Lead on to Wood of Dean;
" Look out for riot," Harry, Jack!
" For hounds are very keen."

Then in they dash, and quest about,
A fox can never rest here;
But hark! a Hound two miles a-head!
No matter that, " 'Tis ' Nestor.'" *

But now, a deep and solemn note
Is heard within the wood:
" 'Tis ' Roe,'" says Jack; " 'Tis *not*," said I,
" 'Tis ' Forester,' the good."

* An incorrigible hare hunter, but afterwards turned out well.

" 'Tis ' Forester,' the good old Hound,
" And hark, hark to his cry ;"
Away they scramble through the brake,
And quickly to him fly.

A whimper from a younger Hound,
Who's rather in a fright,
But " Reginald " and " Lurgan " come,
And quickly set him right.

And now the chorus loud resounds
Throughout the forest glade ;
The fox begins to think that he
Must leave its welcome shade.

Away he goes, and pointing south,
As if for Shores of Forth,
Holds on to Torrie Park, and then
He bends a little north.

Through Oakley Woods and past the house,
He leads a merry dance ;
The owner would have liked the fun,
But he's away in France.

On o'er the railway, up the hill,
And past a farm he speeds ;
" 'Twill put," the farmer loudly shouts,
" My cattle off their feeds."

Blair Wood appears, they do not dwell,
But steady hunt him through ;
Kinneddar's strips and policies
Now burst upon the view.

Across the road to Bandrum Hill,
But here he runs his foil,
A check ensues, we're all at fault,
So round the hill we toil.

A shepherd waves his cap on high,
" The Tod is north !" shouts he,
" The biggest one that e'er I've seen ;
" He's near as long as me !"

Across the road we get a scent,
Yes ! surely that's his line ;
They score to cry ; away they go ;
My certes, but it's fine.

Now " Rioter," he shoots a-head,
Who once was fond of Hare,
But now a fox is scarce afoot,
But " Rioter " is there.

Still up the hill they stream away,
" Excelsior" is the cry ;
And some of us begin to think
Our nags will surely die.

" Come up, good horse, we *will* be there,
" The hill we must get round,"
They cock their ears, their bristles rise,
" We'll have him for a Pound !"

Now cast your eye along yon hedge,
Which leads to Milton Den ;
" 'Tis he ! I see his drooping brush ;
" He's mine for Three Pounds Ten !"

They view him now, and what a rush!
It is a glorious burst;
'Tis "Saffron" now, 'tis "Stormer" yet!
Ah! "Gaylad" has him first.

"Give me a pad," young Oswald cries,
His riding was a caution;
His sister, who went well, is there,
The Brush shall be her portion.

"Give me a pad," George Prentice said,
"To nail upon my door;"
"And me, and me," the others cry,
Alas! he has but four.

"The Hounds all up but one," says Jack,
A Hound of evil habit;
Ha! what's that going o'er the hill?
'Tis "Nestor" with a rabbit!

But we must let him off this time,
Nor whip, nor rate be heard;
'Twould never do to damp our joy—
His punishment's deferred.

And now for home; and though they say
The "Eastern"† pack's the best,
Then come and try, ye Eastern swells,
A gallop with the "West."

From SIR ARTHUR HALKETT.

Pitfirrane, Feb., 1877.

---

† Colonel Anstruther Thomson hunted the East of Fife; Sir Arthur Halkett the West.

LORD GARDNER.

IN the "Sporting Magazine," forty-five years ago, there appeared a poem called " *The Chaunt of Achilles*," concerning the authorship of which no slight curiosity was expressed at the time. The lines in question purported to issue from the bronze lips of the Achilles statue in Hyde Park, and to satirise the appearance, character, and antecedents of all the most conspicuous persons of both sexes who frequented "the Row," upon which the Grecian hero still looks down. Shortly after the death of Mr. Bernal Osborne, some papers were found which seemed to establish that " *The Chaunt of Achilles* " came from his pen, nor is there any lack of internal evidence to show that this surmise, if not correct, is at least not wanting in probability. The anonymous author was certainly of a sarcastic and censorious turn, and among the well-known personages of the day who came under his lash none fared worse or received harder measure than the third Lord Gardner, who died last week. In 1838, when " *The Chaunt of Achilles* " was written, Lord Gardner was in his twenty-ninth year, and had already established for himself the reputation of being one of the best and hardest riders that ever sailed across country with the Quorn or Pytchley hounds. Achilles exclaims—

"But lo! where, following on chesnut dark,
　The grinning Gardner canters down the park,
　Slow in the Senate, though not wanting sense,
　Quick at retort, but quicker at a fence;
　With him no hunter ever dare refuse,
　So good his hand, though damnable his muse.
　Strange, though for years I've listened to the crowd
　Who canvass character, the rich, the proud,

Of him alone I never yet have heard
One kindly action, one approving word.
Sparing of cash, he ne'er outruns the bounds,
And Suffield keeps while Gardner hunts the hounds."

The pack here alluded to was, of course, the Quorn,
which Lord Southampton had given up at the end of
the hunting season of 1830, to be succeeded, first by
Squire Osbaldeston, and then by Lord Suffield. It is a
melancholy reflection that the deaths of Lord Wilton,
of Mr. Stirling Crawfurd, and Lord Gardner, have so
thinned the ranks of the first-flight men who flourished
at Melton about the time when her Majesty ascended
the throne that, with the exception of Mr. Little Gilmour, of Colonel Forester, and of that evergreen veteran,
the Reverend Mr. Bullen,* of Eastwell, there are none
others now left.

Another death has lately taken place—that of a lady
—which reminds us of the vast changes that English
fox-hunting has experienced since the day when, nearly
seventy years ago, the Honourable Barbara Annesley,
great-aunt to the present Lord Valentia, married Squire
Drake, of Shardeloes, who was for many years Master
of the Bicester hounds. What recollections will not
the decease of Mrs. Drake, in her eighty-sixth year,
call up in the minds of many generations of Oxford
undergraduates, who hunted with her husband's hounds
when Plancus was Consul? Within the memory of
many who have scarcely passed middle age, the Peck-
water quadrangle at Christ Church, and the gates of nearly
every other College in Oxford, were alive upon a hunting
morning with cover hacks, upon the backs of which scores of
eager undergraduates proceeded to mount, in order to make

---

* Mr. Bullen is since dead, 1884.

their way at full gallop to Stratton Audley, or Bletching-
ton, or to other well-known meets of Squire Drake's
hounds. Even the strict discipline of Baliol College
when Dr. Jenkins was Master did not restrain the
present Duke of Westminster, the late George Law-
rence, author of "Guy Livingstone," and Sir Henry
Des Vœux, from hunting with Mr. Drake or with the
Heythrop hounds three or four times in every week;
while *University* College habitually sent forth a host of
her sons, with Mr. George Glyn, now Lord Wolverton,
at their head, to try their luck with the Berkshire pack.
When the late Sir Robert Clifton came up to reside at
Christ Church in 1844, he brought fourteen hunters with
him, and in those days the life of an undergraduate,
especially if he was a "tuft," or a gentleman commoner,
differed little from that of a regular habitué of
Melton Mowbray or Market Harborough. The "dons"
did not interfere much with the pleasures and pursuits
of fast and opulent men, so long as they got home
before midnight and slept in college; and it required no
slight amount of ingenuity for an undergraduate to get
rusticated in those easy-going times. It was reserved
for half-a-dozen men belonging to the fast set at Palliol
in 1846 to draw the displeasure of the Master upon
their heads, by riding a steeplechase among themselves,
which led to their being sent down for the rest of the
term. On the Derby Day undergraduates were com-
pelled to dine in hall at five o'clock, so that it should be
impossible for them to attend the great race at Epsom;
but the penalties attached to disobedience did not prevent
Sir Tatton Sykes from going to Epsom in Pyrrhus I.'s
year; the result being that his career as an undergraduate
came prematurely to an end.

The picture of "Melton in 1830," drawn by Lord
Gardner's hand, would not fit the Melton of to-day,

and the fields in which he was a protagonist were small indeed as compared with the swarming hosts of well-mounted men who now attend the meets of the Quorn and Cottesmore hounds. As regards hard riding, we do not believe there is much difference between the best performers of forty and fifty years ago and their successors of to-day. We are told by croakers that the days of fox-hunting are numbered in these sporting islands; but so long as Melton and every other hunting centre boasts the presence of riders who are not inferior to Lord Wilton and Lord Gardner when at their best, we do not expect to see any diminution in the number of packs which take the field in each successive November.

Lord Gardner died November, 1883.

From a newspaper cutting.

HAZLEFORD FERRY:

A TALE OF DISASTER.

FEBRUARY 5TH, 1877.

"The mirth, and the adventure, and the sport that we have shared."

Of those who met at Epperstone on Monday last I tell,
The changes and the chances which that motley crew
   befell;
From the gentlemen in scarlet coats who o'er the fences
   sail
To the little boys on ponies and the tagrag and bobtail.

The north-west wind was blowing on that February
    morn,
And at Thistley when they went away we could not
    hear the horn.
Then such galloping and questioning, such riding and
    such rage,
Till at Thurgarton we find them, and at once our wrath
    assuage.

On to Bleasby, slowly hunting, we come up by twos and
    threes,
And, o'er the ploughs performing, we arrive by slow
    degrees.
From the gorse a change came over the spirit of our
    dream,
As downwards o'er the railway the hounds began to
    stream.

How we cantered, how we galloped, and how down the
    lane we rode;
How we saw the scent improving as a gallant head they
    showed.
I cannot well describe it, for my timid heart beat fast,
When I saw the Trent before us, and I felt the die was
    cast:

One moment in the meadows close beside the flood we
    shrink,
And we anxiously watch Rolleston as he casts them on
    the brink;
But the voices of the bargemen that rise above the roar,
And their cruel gestures show us that he's reached the
    further shore.

The river's running swift and strong, the current it is
    wide,
Yet we must chance the danger—we must reach the
    other side.
So spake each sportsman hardy as he joined the pushing
    mass
That down beside the water scarcely let each other pass.

A sportsman of experience thus to his daughters spoke,
"If we wait till all are over, I can see 'twill be no joke ;
Supposing down the river we were craftily to ride,
Over Fiskerton we rapidly shall reach the other side."

Meanwhile the hounds and huntsmen had been ferried
    o'er the flood,
And their voices, gaily chiming, we could hear beneath
    Stoke Wood,
As we hurried on to Fiskerton with souls intent on sport,
Thinking gladly we should nick them as they down the
    wind turned short.

O! how vexing was that tow-path, with its heavy double
    gates,
And the best of men how trying when about his horse
    he prates.
But at length we reach our ferry—now all difficulty's o'er.
"Hi! boatman! come, look sharp, I say, and punt us
    to yon shore."

Just conceive our indignation, and the blow that we
    were dealt :
"Very sorry, sir ; impossible ; the bottom can't be felt."
Quite remorseless, full of enterprise, we onward dash
    again,
Scarcely thinking, never caring if our errand is in vain.

Fortune seems to smile upon us when we reach the
Farndon shore.
Here's a chain—boat, strong and likely, will hold six
or even more.
With reckless haste we crowd in—seven mortals, horses
five—
With a guilty sense of triumph that we sooner shall
arrive

Than the sportsman of experience who waits the second
turn,
With his daughter sadly watching as their hearts within
them burn.
But ah! what horrid noise is this that breaks upon my
ear ?
A rasping, and a rattling, and a snapping sound I hear.

Then in that laden ferry boat was tumult and affright,
For alas! the chain had broken! we were in a helpless
plight.
With our broadside to the water, while the horses stamp
and snort—
An unpleasant situation, and, you see, with danger
fraught.

So rapidly we glide along the eddying stream straight
down,
It doesn't seem unlikely we shall soon reach Newark
town ;
Unless upon a sand-bank we are left to pass the day
In a sort of picnic party, but without the bill to pay.

But by dint of poles and punting, and of myrmidons
 with ropes,
It appears of landing safely we may entertain good hopes.
But we must take farewell of those we leave the other
 side,
As on the sodden grass we leap with thankfulness and
 pride.

Now after such adventures and disasters who could
 guess
That we found our trouble wasted—was there ever such
 a mess?
We galloped down the old Foss road, we galloped o'er
 the plough,
But hounds and huntsman all are gone—we cannot hear
 them now.

The gallant fox swam back, they say, and lives to run
 again,
And if we're there to hunt him we'll forgive the broken
 chain.
The sportsmen on the other side who saw the evening's
 run
With us will wish these hounds good luck and "years
 of future fun."

L. C. M.

THE RUFFORD HOUNDS.

Sir,—On Tuesday, Nov. 29, these hounds had a
remarkable run, which will long be remembered by those
who were fortunate enough to see it, and which has

never been surpassed in the annals of fox-hunting in
the Rufford country. The meet was at Caunton Manor,
and, after the usual chat with Canon Hole, who loves
fox-hunting, as does his good lady, the Master decided
to draw Werner Wood instead of Caunton Park (where
the Canon can generally find as good a fox as most
folks). His reason for so doing was that Werner
Wood held twice this season a wild fox who was off
before hounds were fairly in the covert. On this occasion the Master viewed him away just as Hayes was
about throwing his hounds (the dog pack) into the wood,
and soon every hound was on his line and away for
Caunton Park, where he did not dwell a moment, but
held on to Ossington High Wood. Just before reaching
this covert a sheep-dog coursed him, and hounds checked,
as they always do when these brutes interfere; but
Hayes hit him off into the wood, and, getting a holloa
away from Harry on the other side, was soon at Knee-
sall Green Wood. Through this covert hounds hunted
him steadily and well, and again was he viewed away by
Harry pointing for Wellow Park; but, turning short of
it, he ran through Pinder's Farm, and made as if for
Kirton Wood, turned down the hill into the village, and
hounds nearly had him in the orchards, but he slipped
through a yard and over the fine grass meadows and
the brook, which proved fatal to more than one, and a
bridge breaking in likewise, the field was considerably
reduced, and set his head straight for the forest, hounds
running hard over Boughton Brake, and through the
small covert alongside the river, past Conger Alders,
over the Retford-road, as if for Patmore, in Lord
Galway's country, but his strength was failing, and soon
the Master viewed him struggling on before the hounds,
who were now running for their fox past Peck's Farm,

through Blyth Corner, into Clumber, where again he is
viewed by Hayes, who was, as he invariably is, close to
his hounds, and just before they reached the boundary
of the Rufford country, the hounds (whose work from
beginning to end had been beyond all praise) ran into
him in fine style close to the Clumber Nurseries, and
not a stone's throw from Normanton Inn. A select
few, good men and true every one, saw this grand old
fox given to the good hounds, who so well deserved
him, and all turned homewards, believing they had seen
such a run as they could hardly hope to see again.
With a long experience of the country, I may say that
I never remember a "clay" fox coming so far into the
forest, and I never recollect scent being equally good
on both "clay" and "sand." The distance as the crow
flies is twelve miles, as they ran, fourteen. Time, one
hour and fifty minutes.

SHERWOOD FOREST. (T. H. D. B.)

THE GLORY OF MOTION:

SOUTH OXFORDSHIRE.

Three twangs of the horn, and they're all out of cover—
Must have yon old bullfinch, that's right in the way:
A rush, and a bound, and a crash, and I'm over;
They're silent, and racing, and for'ard away!
Fly, Charley, my darling! away and we follow!
There's no earth or cover for mile upon mile;
We're winged with the flight of the stork and the
    swallow—
The heart of the eagle is ours for a while.

The pasture land knows not of rough plough or harrow,
The hoofs echo hollow and soft on the sward;
The soul of the horses goes into our marrow—
My saddle's the kingdom, whereof I am lord;
And, rolling and flowing beneath us like ocean,
Gray waves of the high ridge and furrow glide on;
And small flying fences, in musical motion,
Before us, beneath us, behind us, are gone.

Oh, puissant of bone and of sinew availing,
To speed through the glare of the long desert hours;
My white-breasted camel, the meek and unfailing,
That sighed not, like me, for the shades and the showers;
And bright little Barbs, with veracious pretences
To blood of the Prophet's and Solomon's sires;
You stride not the stride, and you fly not the fences,
And all the wide Hejaz is naught to the Shires.

O, gay gondolier! from thy night-flitting shallop
I've heard the soft pulses of oar and guitar;
But sweeter 's the rhythmical rush of the gallop,
The "fire in the saddle," the flight of the star.
Old mare, my beloved, no stouter or faster
Hath ever strode under a man at his need:
Be glad in the hand and embrace of thy master,
And pant to the passionate music of speed.

Old Beauty—how quickly, as onward she races
And "comes through her horses" in spite of my hold,
I catch the expression of jolly brown faces
Of parties a-going it over the wold.
They mostly look anxiously glad to be in it,
All hitting, and holding, and bucketing past;
O, pleasure of pleasures! from minute to minute—
The pace and the horses—may both of them last.

Can there e'er be a thought to an elderly person
So keen, so inspiring—so hard to forget—
So fully adapted to break into verse on
As this—that the steel isn't out of him yet?
That flying speed tickles one's brain with a feather;
That one's horse can restore one the years that are gone;
That spite of gray winter and weariful weather,
The blood and the pace carry on, carry on!

> R. St. John Tyrwhitt,
> In "Our Sketching Club."

"FORMOSISSIMUS ANNUS."

Autumn, 1884.

They have done with the beans, they have carried the
    corn,
The white Autumn furrows are glittering and shorn;
The seven-o'clock sunshine is cloudless and clear,
And sweet to the end is the Beautiful Year.

The Port Meadow turf echoes low as we ride,
And light is the gallop by Isis her side;
Down float on her waters, more scarlet than sere,
The sun-tinted leaves of the Beautiful Year.

Black rooks and grey starlings are mustering on high,
The blue heron wings over with desolate cry;
The lapwings they whistle and wail far and near;
Are they sad for the wane of the Beautiful Year?

Not they—nor we either—in Wytham once more
The O. B. are out, with a stout cub before;
Push up the long hill thro' the cover, and hear
Their earliest chime, in the Beautiful Year.

Sweet birds and light leaves—ye may glitter and fly:
We send a sigh after, but only a sigh:
Thy death has a beauty that casteth out fear
With hope in thine ending, O Beautiful Year.

R. St. J. T.

HOW WE BEAT THE FAVOURITE.

" Ay, Squire," said George Stevens, " they back him at
    evens—
  The race is all over bar shouting, they say :
The Clown ought to beat her—Dick Neville is sweeter
  Than ever; he swears he can win all the way."

A gentleman rider! well, I'm an outsider;
  But if he's a gent, who the deuce is a jock?
Your swells mostly blunder—Dick rides for the plunder;
  He rides, too, like thunder—he sits like a rock.

He calls "hunted fairly" a horse that has barely
  Been stripped for a trot within sight of the hounds;
A horse that at Warwick beat Birdlime and Yorick,
  And gave Abdel Kader at Aintree nine pounds.

They say we have no test to warrant a protest:
  Dick rides for a lord, and stands in with a steward.
The light of their faces they show him his case is
  Prejudged, and his verdict already secured.

But none can outlast her, and few travel faster ;
　　She strides in her work clean away from " the Drag."
You hold her and sit her—she couldn't be fitter—
　　Whenever you hit her she'll spring like a stag.

And perhaps the green jacket, tho' at odds they may
　　　back it,
　　May fall, or there's no knowing what may turn up.
The mare is just ready—sit still and ride steady ;
　　Keep cool, and I think you may just win the cup.

Dark brown with tan muzzle, just stripped for the tuzzle,
　　Stood Iseult, now arching her neck to the curb :
A lean head and fiery, strong quarters and wiry ;
　　A loin rather light, but a shoulder superb.

Some parting injunction, bestowed with great unction,
　　I tried to recall, but forgot like a dunce,
When Reginald Murray, full tilt on White Surrey,
　　Came down in a hurry to start us at once.

" Keep back, in the yellow !"　" Come up, on Othello !"
　　" Hold hard, on the chesnut !"　" Turn round on the
　　　Drag !"—
" Keep back there, on Spartan !"　" Back you, sir, in
　　　tartan !"
　　" So, steady there, easy !" and down went the flag.

We started—and Kerr made strong running on Mermaid
　　Through furrows that led to the first stake and bound ;
The crack, half extended, looked blood-like and splendid,
　　Held wide on the right, where the headland was sound.

The fourth fence—a wattle—floored Monk and Blue-
    bottle—
The Drag came to grief at the black thorn and ditch.
The rails toppled over Redoubt and Red Rover—
    The lane stopped Lycurgus and Leicestershire Witch.

She passed like an arrow Kildare and Cock Sparrow,
    And Mantrap and Mermaid refused the stone wall;
And Giles on the Grayling came down at the paling,
    And I was left sailing in front of them all.

I took them a burster—nor eased her, nor nursed her
    Until the black bullfinch led into the plough;
And thro' the strong bramble we bored with a scramble—
    My cap was knocked off by a hazel tree bough.

Where furrows looked lighter I pulled the rein tighter,
    The dark chest all dappled with flakes of white foam;
The flanks mud bespattered—a weak rail we shattered—
    We land on the turf with our heads turned for home.

She cracked a low binder, and then close behind her
    The sward to the hoofs of the favourite shook.
His rush roused her mettle, yet ever so little—
    She shortened her stride as we raced for the brook.

She rose when I hit her—I saw the stream glitter—
    A wide scarlet nostril pushed close to my knee.
Between sky and water the Clown came and caught
    her,
    The space that he cleared was a caution to see.

And forcing the running, discarding all cunning,
  A length to the front went the rider in green.
A long strip of stubble, and then the big double—
  Two stiff flights of rails, with a quickset between.

She raced at the rasper—I felt my knees grasp her;
  I found my hands give to the strain on the bit.
She rose when the Clown did—our silks as we bounded
  Brushed lightly—our stirrups clashed loops as we hit.

Arise, steeply sloping, a fence with stone coping—
  The last: we diverged round the base of the hill.
His path was the nearer—his leap was the clearer—
  I flogged up the straight, and he led sitting still.

She came to his quarter, and on still I brought her,
  And up to his girths and his breast-plate she drew.
A short prayer from Neville just reached me—"the
    devil!"
  He muttered—locked level, the hurdles we flew.

A hum of hoarse cheering—a dense crowd careering—
  All sights seen obscurely—all shouts vaguely heard:
"The green wins!" "the crimson!" the multitude
    swims on:
  The figures are blended—the features are blurred.

"The horse is her master!" "the green forges past her!"
  "The Clown will outlast her—the Clown wins! the
    Clown!"
The white railing races, with all the white faces—
  The chesnut outpaces, outstretches the brown!

On still past the gateway, she strains in the straight-
way—
   Still struggles the " Clown by a short neck at most : "
He swerves! the green scourges—the stand rocks and
   surges,
And flashes, and verges, and flits the white post.

Ay, so ends the struggle.   I knew the tan muzzle
   Was first, tho' the ring-men were yelling dead heat.
A nose I could swear by, but the judge said, " the mare
   by
   A short head," and that's how the favourite was beat.

             From MAJOR PAGET MOSLEY.

NOTES FROM WILL STANSBY'S DIARY AT BADMINTON, 1843.

Amongst ye changes this spring are ye following :—
April.—Ye East Sussex hounds sold for debt.   Lord
Ducie bought most of them, and gave to Lord Giffard.

The first whip from ye Quorn, B. Boothroyd, goes
as huntsman to the Marquis of Hastings, succeeding
Will Derry, who goes to hunt Lord Southampton's,
vice Taylor.

Charles Treadwell leaves Mr. Robertson, and goes to
hunt Earl of Harewood's.

Mr. Robertson, of Lady Kirk, gives up ye Northumberland country, and sells his pack to Lord Elcho, who
resigns East Lothian to hunt ye country vacated by
Mr. R. in Berwickshire.   I hear the distemper has
been very favourable with Lord Elcho this year, not

having yet lost one young hound. They put forward 22 couples.

F. Flint leaves Lord Southampton (first whip), and goes to hunt the Duke of Cleveland's stag hounds. He lived some years with the Duke of Rutland as first whip, and left on Goosey's retirement from ye post of huntsman, and Goodall's (Wm.) promotion from second whip to Goosey's place, in ye spring, 1842.

The Norfolk hounds given up this spring through scarcity of foxes and want of support.

Lord Portman gives up his "wee" pack, which are bought by Earl Shannon to hunt in Ireland, in addition to what he bought of Lord Bruce, and hunted in Ireland with last season. Thos. Bown went to him last season as huntsman, or rather latter end of ye summer. He had lived with Sir Thomas Stanley.

Mr. Cockburn gives up ye Tiverton country (Devon), and takes ye Hursley country, Hants.

Charles Bridges goes from Badminton as second whip to the Duke of Rutland.

The past season, the Heythrop hounds had most excellent sport. Captain Anstey told William Long, in my hearing, that it was worth any two seasons he ever remembered to have seen.

Earl Fitzhardinge's killed 76½ brace of foxes; but Harry Ayris told me they had not a succession of sport; in short, that it was with them a very indifferent season. More blood I never heard tell of any one pack getting in one season.

William Todd, at ye beginning of ye past season, went to Sir Richard Sutton as huntsman, on Shirley giving up, and Sir Richard taking ye Cottesmore country. He, however, soon left, and went back to Mr. Harvey Coombe (whose hounds he had been hunting in

the old Berkeley country) as groom. Sir Richard had
a very unfavourable season indeed. Great complaints.
I saw a letter from Mr. Gilmour to John Campbell,
Esq., of Glensaddel, wherein he says the hounds seldom
find their fox, but are daily halloo'd to them after drawing the coverts ; instancing one day in particular, when
they drew Woodall Head,* a very favourite covert,
without finding. On leaving it they were halloo'd back,
a fox having been viewed in ye covert. On their taking
to ye scent, a brace more, making a leash, were proved
to be there. " This," says he, " occurs daily."

Mr. Campbell, after hunting with the Duke of
Beaufort, at whose house he stayed ye season, sold his
stud of eight horses at Tattersall's, excepting that rare
old horse Paganini, which was taken back to Scotland,
and afterwards sold to J. O. Fairlie, Esq.

Friday, September 9th, 1842.—Duke of Beaufort's
hounds.—Killcott. Ye morning very wet and stormy.
Went home at nine o'clock. At half-past ten went out
on ye lawn with 22½ couple fresh hounds, to draw Swan
Grove, ye Duke, Prince Leichtenstein, and several
foreigners, being at Badminton. Ye day turned out
very wet; and as it was intended for a day for ye
Princess and ladies, postponed till ye morrow.

Saturday, Sept. 10th, 1842.—Met on ye lawn 22½
couple. Went to Swan Grove. Found a brace of
mangy foxes; had some little running backwards and
forwards, and finally killed one in ye gorse by Ragged
Castle. Went to Bodkin Wood. Found at least 3
brace of cubs; killed a brace in covert; went away with
a third over ye corner of ye Park piece to Badminton
Village, by ye green pond into ye Vicarage, nearly to

---

* Woodwell Head.

ye pleasure ground; got in ye ditch, jumped out in view, and soon killed. Three couple of hounds had been left at Bodkin Wood. James Watts, the feeder, got them away. Met a fox in Mr. Sydney's turnips. Frankfort seized and nearly killed him; took him home alive. A single hound, aided by numerous bipeds, caught another in ye Park piece, whilst trying to get in a drain. Sent him back sound to Bodkin Wood. This was an eventful and butchering day. Prince Leichtenstein and Princess, Count Esterhazy, Baron Nieuman, &c., out. I thought ye Princess Leichtenstein the finest woman I ever saw, and handsome withal.

Wednesday, January 11th, 1843.—Iron Acton. Eighteen couple dogs. Draw'd Parsons Wood, ye Marl Pits, &c. No fox. Came on to Yate Rocks; drew ye Coombe, and both Brinsham coverts, and Maple rudge. No fox. Got on a scent in Bays; hunted over ye Broad Trench; got up to a brace of foxes in Horton side. Hounds divided for a few minutes; got together, recrossed ye Trench, thro' Bays and Bedfords; very quick over ye brook, and up ye hill nearly to ye turnpike road, to ye left by Bird's Bush, crossing ye road by Mr. Goodwyn's into ye vale below; bore to ye left thro' the Coombe, and over ye wood again by ye lime kiln at Yate Rocks, skirting ye lesser Brinsham covert, to ye Maple rudge bushes; to ye right and away, at a good pace, across ye vale under Horton, nearly to Chalkley; bore a little to ye right, leaving ye old mansion and Horton Church close on ye right; up ye hill, thro' ye Walk Wood, and on for Bodkin Hazle, running ye green lane nearly to ye end of ye covert, just entered, and away over ye Bath road, thro' Bodkin Wood, and on towards Little Badminton; bore to the left, pointing for Swan Grove, was headed,

back touching Bodkin Wood, near Petty France, and
back thro' ye Hazle. I viewed him from hence, some
distance, apparently in difficulty—ye hounds following steadily thro' ye covert on his line, did not get
so quick away as I could have wished. On leaving
Chalkley on ye left, into ye vale again, when we had a
check of two or three minutes, hit off, and went a good
pace over ye lower end of Hawkesbury Common into
Littley, and up ye woods to ye further end of Maple
rudge, back along ye covert towards Bays. 1 here
viewed ye fox away, and was damped to find we had
changed our fox; hunted down into Bays, and stopped
ye hounds. Very good day's sport—worth 1000 of your
10, 12, or 15 minutes' skurries to a lover of hunting.
Mr. Campbell, Mr. J. Bailey, and Mr. R. Kingscote
went as well or rather better than any other; Mr.
Campbell screaming in raptures as we got near Bodkin
Hazle. Blood only was wanting to render this run all
that could be wished by a sportsman.

(Long) L.	(Stansby) S.	C. (Chas. Bridges)
Milkman	Marion	Gamecock
Archduke	Etonian	Miss Tree

1845.—This season we have an addition to our
country of Stoke Gifford coverts, &c., conceded by Earl
Fitzhardinge. Though some of them ye Duke of Beaufort's property, they have been hitherto a part of ye
Berkeley hunt. Rood Ashton, near Troubridge, also
belonging to Walter Long, Esq., and hitherto hunted
by Mr. Horlock, is now to be hunted by the Duke of
Beaufort.

There was an immense quantity of corn grown this
year. The spring was everything that could be desired;
crops most luxuriant; in fact, I believe most people
will admit that they never remember to have seen the

land so heavily covered with both hay and corn. Ye early hay harvest was good, but the July month was very wet and cold, and also the first week in August; and there is yet (although ye bulk of corn is housed in ye best possible condition) a good deal of wheat and barley not only in ye field, but uncut. (September 23rd.) Beans are famous crops. Nuts plentiful; acorns scarce. Potatoes infested with a disease throughout ye country, and ye price of corn kept up in consequence.

When I was a lad in the stables at Calke, in 1817, 1818, 1819, on the door of a passage, in the N.E. corner of the stable yard, were the plates of several race-horses nailed to the door, and a name under each. I think there were five of them. I remember one of Dairymaid, one of Mixbury, one of Juniper, and one of the famous Skewball. The names were cut in the wood, apparently with a knife; and I fancied these horses must have stood in this stable, and belonged to the Sir Harry Harpur, Bart., of that day; and I used to look on the plates with considerable interest, and longed to know something about them. Many years after, and far away from Calke, I heard several times a doggerel song in praise of Skewball. I used to listen to it attentively, as it recalled to my memory the plate with his name on the old door where I strapped many an hour with a wet shirt. Since then I found the following in the Sporting Magazine of May, 1834:—
"Skewball foaled in 1741. Bred by the Earl of Godolphin. Sold to Sir Harry Harpur, Bart., at whose death he was purchased by Lord Robert Sutton Manners. His next master was Mr. Elston, who disposed of him to Arthur Mervin, Esq., who raced him in Ireland, where he beat Sir Ralph Gore's grey mare by

Victorious over the Curragh of Kildare for 300 guineas each, and was also the winner of a great number of plates and prizes.

June, 1843.—William Collins, of Badminton, labourer, aged 83 years, hearty, having the use of all his faculties, and working on ye road, tells me he can remember when foxes were destroyed at Badminton, ye keepers being paid for it; that ye Duke of that day kept stag hounds and harriers, and that the deer were penned at Oldham-on-the-Hill. That he remembers all ye huntsmen, as under :—

Baldwin
Wilts   }   Stag hounds, &c.
Hellier

Crane (began keeping foxhounds—a heavy man).
Kench.   Alderton.   Dilworth.
Philip Payne.   William Long.

Then followed the 8th Duke of Beaufort and William Stansby, Thomas Clarke in 1858, and left somewhat suddenly before the close of the season 1867—1868. The Marquis of Worcester then took the horn.

A LEGEND OF GALWAY.

From the gorse of Ahascragh* the hounds broke away,
With the "grey fox" on foot and a warm scenting day.
The cracks of Roscommon are here, and they swear,
Come life or come death, to beat Valentine Maher. †

He's last thro' the clay and the deep of the vale,
Not seen at the gap in the third post and rail ;
And, still with the lead, the Roscommons ask, " where
Is the pride of your country, bold Valentine Maher ? "

Then, smiling aside, the old huntsman spoke low,
" With the grey fox on foot we've a day's work to do ;
You'll have nerves of the strongest, nor steel must you
        spare
If you ride to the finish with Valentine Maher."

All the while his hot chestnut was chafing in vain,
Till the foam from her nostrils speck'd breastplate and rein ;
But cool, as at first, " take your time, never care ;
We'll catch 'em yet, Kathleen," said Valentine Maher.

---

* Ahascragh, Lord Clonbrock's place in Galway.

"Many thanks for sending me the Legend of Galway. The lines read very spirited, and make one fancy a bygone delusion, viz., chancing it at a rasper. Valentine Maher carries me back to the days of my childhood. I recollect so well when he came to stay with my father at Stapleford, and after that he came to Glaston on his way to Newmarket, making his journey to the turf metropolis on foot.
                                "SIR THOMAS WHICHCOTE, Jan., 1884."

†Valentine Maher, of Turtulla, Co. Tipperary, and M.P. for that County. Born 1780 ; died 1844, unmarried.

"One of the leading men on these occasions (viz., "larking") is Mr. Maher, a brilliant performer with hounds ; but without hounds, in Leicestershire, few men have a chance with him, from his perfect knowledge of the country. On the Widmerpool day, of which I have been speaking, he led about a dozen of them a dance ol upwards of nine miles. over a beautiful country, in little more than half an hour."—NIMROD, in Sporting Magazine, 1825.

They near'd the Black River, they heard its dull roar—
They mark'd the thick mist-wreaths that brood on its
    shore;
When his laugh, close behind them, rang cheery and
    clear—
" Here's food for the fishes," quoth Valentine Maher.

While they stood on the bank, and the boldest held
    breath
As he gazed on the torrent, three fathoms beneath;
When the best of Roscommon drew rein in despair,
With a rush to the front came Valentine Maher.

He called upon Kathleen—one snort and one spring,
She clove thro' the air like a swallow on wing.
He turn'd in his saddle—"now, follow who dare!
I ride for my country," quoth Valentine Maher.

The hounds left the valley—they strain'd up the hill—
But one rider remains, and he sticks to them still.
They check'd on the brow of Kilconnel, and there,
To turn them and cast them, was Valentine Maher.

Where the coverts of pine over Athenry frown,
Within one mile of home, the grey fox was pulled down;
And rock, hill, and valley sent back the death cheer,
As they rang to the halloo of Valentine Maher.

So we'll drink with nine cheers to the old county's breed—
To the blood in the veins of both rider and steed;
And here's, " The next time that Roscommon shall dare
Go straight across Galway with Valentine Maher!"

AUTHOR OF " GUY LIVINGSTONE."

THE LOVER'S LEAP.

Quid Fœmina Possit.

Well, though I love not boasting,
  Sith all will have it so,
You shall hear how we left the field behind
  A score of years ago.

Time will unclasp his fetters,
  And age grow young once more,
When we think of all that was dared and done
  In the mad days of yore.

But, first fill up another cup
  Till o'er the mantled brim,
Sweet as the dew of a red ripe lip,
  The glittering bubbles swim:

"To the loving and the lov'd" we'll drink,
  "The frank, the kind, the bold;
To all warm living hearts, and those
  That never till death were cold."

'Twas a dull November morning,
  South wind and cloudy sky,
When, if scent were ever certain,
  A fox was doom'd to die.

We met at Bolton Thicket,
  That never blank was drawn;
Fresh lies the scene before me now
  As it were but yester'-morn.

Ten acres of copse, on a gentle slope,
　By a belt of gorse surrounded;
All grass, as far as the eye could reach,
　By the low, blue hill-line bounded.

That day my mount was Thunderbolt,
　Of black Prunella's breed,
Who, thro' toil and peril never yet
　Had fail'd me at my need;
With strength for the deep, and wind for the down,
　With a racing turn of speed.

Ere long a challenge and a cheer
　Came floating down the wind,
'Twas Mermaid's note, and the huntsman's voice—
　We knew it was a find.
The dull air woke as from a trance,
　As sixty hounds joined chorus;
And away we went, with a stout dog fox
　Not a furlong's length before us.

A quiver shot through my strong horse
　From his hoof to his swelling crest,
As a stout ship thrusts the waves aside,
　Thro' the meaner crowd he prest,
Till he took the place that was his by right,
　And we settled down in the foremost flight
To hold our own with the best.

The sight of a hound or the sound of a horn
　Warms my old blood even now,
And this was when the tide of youth
　Ran foaming at its flow—
No trifle in those merry days
　Turn'd me and my peers I trow!

Yet a shudder, such as cowards feel,
    Thro' my very marrow crept,
When I saw a fence that cross'd our line,
    As down the hill we swept :

And well the firmest cheek might blanch,
    The sternest courage fail
At the bullfinch, with its yawning drain,
    A deep drop into a stony lane,
And a four-foot oaken rail.

Each look'd on each, till thus spoke out
    The Nestor of our band,
A veteran of war and chase
    Who rode at my right hand :

" The churl who yonder man-trap laid
    By an ill-death may he fall !
If the fox has headed across the road
    The hounds will leave us all ;
For a tougher brush it were to face
    Yon blackthorn's venomed spears,
Than ever we had in the olden time
    With Kellermann's cuirassiers.

In the pasture just below us
    A knot of gazers stood,
Whose eyes had never left us
    Since we broke from Bolton Wood.
The best blood of two counties
    Made up that bright array,
And there the queen of all our hearts
    Sate on her fiery grey.

E

Hither and thither rode the field,
　　Seeking an easier place—
I, too, had turned me, when I met
　　My mistress face to face:
I bounded in my seat like one
　　Death-stricken thro' the brain—
Sweet wife! the bliss of after years
　　Scarce paid that instant's pain.

There was scorn upon her curling lip,
　　In her dark eyes angry flame,
On the marble of her polish'd brow
　　Red rose the flush of shame.

The veriest dastard had grown brave
　　There—face to face with her:
I bit my lip through as I wheel'd,
　　And drove home either spur.

Sprang to the steel old Thunderbolt,
　　And snorted savagely;
The blood-gouts dripp'd from his dusky sides
　　Like rain from a low'ring sky:
I felt as I rush'd him at the fence
　　He was as wild as I.

Then came, too late, a warning shriek,
　　And then such crackling sound
As echoes through a burning house
　　When beams are splint'ring round.

But o'er crash and cry, rose clear and high
　　The voice well loved and known,
Though not a silver note was strain'd—
　　" O Charlie! bravely done."

Of six score men, there was but one
  To follow where I led—
Good faith! his daring cost him dear,
  For as I turn'd my head,
He was writhing 'neath his mare, who lay
  With a broken neck, stone dead.

No time to pause, for over the meads
  We swept, with a scent breast-high;
Six more good miles we carried it on,
  The brave bitch pack and I.

And when we turned him up, my cheer,
  Borne on the rising wind,
Came faintly to the nearmost ear,
  A long half league behind.

'Twas a cold November evening,
  And the homeward way was dreary;
For a score of miles before us lay,
  And man and horse were weary.

But my heart was warm as I thought of the smile
  That my return would greet,
When she heard the story of the day,
  With its trophy at her feet.

AUTHOR OF "GUY LIVINGSTONE."

THE CHARLTON HUNT.

SOME years since, in an old farm-house at Funtington, in West Sussex, a precious document was discovered; relating to the Charlton Hunt, and consisting of a manuscript account of a run with the hounds. Commencing with a heading, it is as follows:—

"A FULL AND IMPARTIAL ACCOUNT OF THE REMARKABLE CHASE AT CHARLTON, ON FRIDAY, 26TH JAN., 1738.

"Present in the morning: the Duke of Richmond, the Duchess of Richmond, Duke of St. Albans, Lord Harcourt, the Lord Henry Beauclerk, the Lord Ossulston, Sir Harry Liddell, Brigadier Henry Hawley, Ralph Jennison, Master of His Majesty's buckhounds, Edward Pauncefoot, Esq., William Farquhar, Esq., Cornet Philip Honeywood, Richard Biddulph, Esq., Charles Biddulph, Esq., Mr. St. Paul, Mr. Johnson, Billy Ives, yeoman pricker to His Majesty's hounds, David Briggs and Ninn Ives, whippers-in.

"At a quarter before eight in the morning the fox was found in East Dean Wood, and ran an hour in that cover, then in the Forest up to Puntice Copse, through Heringdean to the Marlows, to Covey Coppice, back to the Marlows, to the Forest West Gate, over the fields to Nightingale Bottom, to Cobden's Draught, up his Pine Pit Hanger, where his Grace of St. Albans got a fall; through West Dean Forest to the corner of Collar Down (where Lord Harcourt blew his first horse), crossed the Hackney-place Down, the length of Colney Coppice, through the Marlows to Heringdean, into the Forest and Puntice Coppice, East Dean Wood, through the lower Teglease, across by Cocking Course, down

between Graffham and Woolavington; through Mr.
Orme's park and paddock, over the heath to Fielding's
Furzes, to the Hurlands, Selham, Ambersham, through
Todham Furzes, over Todham Heath, almost to Cow-
dray Park, there turned to the limekiln at the end of
Cocking Causeway, through Cocking Park and Furzes,
there crossed the road, and up the hills between Bepton
and Cocking. Here the unfortunate Lord Harcourt's
second horse felt the effects of long legs and a sudden
steep. The best thing that belonged to him was his
saddle, which my lord had secured; but by bleeding
and Geneva (contrary to Act of Parliament), he recovered, and was with some difficulty got home. Here
Mr. Farquhar's humanity claims your regard, who
kindly sympathised with my lord in his misfortunes, and
had not power to go beyond him. At the bottom of
Cocking Warren the hounds turned to the left, across
the road, by the barn, near Heringdean, then took the
side to the north gate of the Forest (here General
Hawley thought it prudent to change his horse for a true
blue that staid up the hills. Billy Ives also took a horse
of Sir Harry Liddell); went quite through the Forest;
went through the Warren above West Dean (where we
dropped Sir Harry Liddell), through Goodwood Park
(here the Duke of Richmond chose to send three lame
horses back to Charlton, and took Saucy Face and Sir
William, that were luckily at Goodwood; from there,
at a distance, Lord Harry was seen driving his horse
before him to Charlton). The hounds went out at the
upper end of the park, over Strettington road, by Scaly
Coppice (where his Grace of Richmond got a summerset),
through Halnaker Park, over Halnaker Hill, to Seabeach
Farm (here the master of the staghounds, Cornet
Honeywood, Tom Johnson, and Ninn Ives, were

thoroughly satisfied), up Long Down, through Eartham Common Fields, and Kemp's High Woods (here Billy Ives hired his second horse, and took Sir William, by which the Duke of St. Albans had no greatcoat, so returned to Charlton). From Kemp's High Wood the hounds took away through Gunworth Warren, Kent Rough Piece, over Slindon down to Madehurst Parsonage (where Billy came in with them), over Poor Down up to Madehurst, then down to Houghton Forest, where his Grace of Richmond, General Hawley, and Mr. Pouncefoot came in (the latter to little purpose, for, beyond the Race Hill, neither Mr. Pauncefoot nor his horse, Tinker, cared to go, so wisely returned to his impatient friends); up the Race Hill, left Sherwood on the right hand, crossed Offham Hill to Southwood; from thence to South Stoke, to the wall of Arundel River, where the glorious twenty-three hounds put an end to the campaign, and killed an old bitch fox, ten minutes before six. Billy Ives, his Grace of Richmond, and General Hawley, were the only persons in at the death, to the immortal honour of seventeen stone, and at least as many campaigns."

The Charlton Hunt came to an end, and the kennel was removed for a short time to Goodwood, afterwards to Petworth, whose owner, Lord Leconfield, is still the M.F.H. of his locality.

H. E. IN "FORESTRY."

HUNTING SONG FOR THE YEAR 1824.

I am a jolly huntsman, and rise before 'tis day;
Let loose my dogs, and mount my horse, and halloo
   come away.
        And a hunting we will go.

Of all our fond diversions a hunter's is the best;
In spite of wars and party jars the sport is to the test.

Brisk action cures the vapours, th' effects of lazy sloth,
And music makes us cheerful, so hunting's good for both.

Of Nimrod and of Esau what mighty feats they tell—
On foot they followed hunting, they loved the sport so
well.

Had Dido not loved hunting, the amorous Trojan brave
Her Highness ne'er had solaced in Juno's friendly cave.

Eurypides! had hunting been minded like thy books
The hounds had ne'er devoured thee—they know a
sportsman's looks;

And hadst thou, brave Actæon, have minded but thy game,
Thou ne'er hadst paid so dearly for peeping at the same.

Orion, foolish hunter, lured by a petticoat,
In the mid chase he loitered, and so his fate he got.

But after this disaster he's made a heavenly sign,
That he at least may view the sport he can no longer join.

The British King's* a hunter, and frequent in the chase;
He minds no more than we do a weather-beaten face.

Then fill your sparkling glasses, and take them off with
glee—
"Here's to all brother sportsmen, in course His
Majesty."   And a hunting we will go.
                    SPORTING MAGAZINE, 1825.

---

* King George the Third.

A RUN WITH THE S. O.,

AND A WORD ON PARSONS HUNTING.

IT was, I believe, in November, 1873, (when I was clergyman at Albury, and possessed of an old roaring dun mare, a capital fencer, but not particularly fast,) that the hounds met at the Three Pigeons, one of their Monday meets. It was in my parish, and I always went to the meet when they met in the parish.

We had a little run in the morning, and about one o'clock got away with a big fox from Fernhill, a cover which was just opposite my house, and had some strong earths. I knew this old fox, having seen him about on the glebe. The foxes used to come all round my house. I have had them after the fowl at eleven o'clock in the middle of the day—the fowl all flying on the roof of the house—and quite late in the day. There was a fox in the stable yard one evening about eight o'clock. I generally had a litter in my own plantation near the church. The big fox crossed the rail close under Albury, across the Draycot and Waterstock Meadows, crossed the river Thames under Waterperry House (Mr. Henley's)—the field crossing by Waterstock Bridge—and so into Waterperry Wood, by Park Farm; crossed the road into Hell Copse, and so into the quarters. I went down to the corner of the big wood, Shabbington Wood, towards Worminghall village, and while standing there with Mr. Bull, of Albury, saw something go away two fields off. I rode as hard as I could for a better view, but though I was almost sure it was a fox, dare not halloa without being certain. After waiting about ten minutes or a quarter of an hour, the hounds came down on his line—the field soon got round after the hounds, for we got away very slowly, the fox having been gone so long, and well we did; for, after crossing the Oakley and Worminghall road, the fences were very big, one or two being boreable and not jumpable; but after leaving Oakley on the left, the scent improved in the big grass meadows under Brill, and we had to gallop to keep with hounds. What beautiful meadows those are! We crossed the Chilton and Dorton road, close to Dorton, and down to the Chearsley brook, where there was a good deal of grief. I and three others were riding rather wide on the right, and we had it at a good place. George Castle first, Lady Adelaide Parker second, a man on a cob third, and I fourth. I could see it was something big by the way George Castle and Lady Adelaide went at it. My dear old father got in higher up on Baronet, an old horse he had bought of Lord Macclesfield, and which Lady Adelaide rode for six seasons; and he then had a post rail, which he rode at three times before he got over. Colonel Ruck Keene told me afterwards that he halloed to my father, "I hope I shall ride like that when I am your age." And so to Chearsley Gorse, where we did not check above two or three minutes; back over almost the same line to the brook—but this time nearer the bridge to Chearsley village—which I believe nearly all went over, and then up the hill to Chilton village very fast, the hounds almost racing away from us. I remember going up one fence, looking for a weak place, but it kept getting bigger, and at last I turned at it in despair, my father following. He said afterwards it was a very big place. We checked at Chilton village for a minute or two, and then ran on to Chinkwell Wood, under Brill Hill, where they lost him, going to ground, I think.

The distance from the woods was not so very great, and we may very likely have changed in them; but the hounds never ceased running after leaving Fernhill. My dear old father did not leave Oxford very early, and just came up as we were getting away. How he did enjoy it. He would sometimes come out for half a day in the afternoon, having his horse to meet him at the door of the schools (the old schools under the Bodleian library). Old Baronet was then eighteen, and went well. Lord Macclesfield said that day, " If I had known he could go like that, you never should have had him." My father had him for three years, but he fell and broke two of his ribs, larking in Wytham Park, over some of Lord Norreys' made-up fences, and then he came to me for three years more, and taught my wife to ride, before he went to his old home at the kennels.

The distance from Fernhill to Chinkwell Wood, as we ran, is about 15½ miles by the ordnance map, but from the corner of Shabbington Wood to Chinkwell, about nine miles, via Chearsley and Chilton, and this was the best of the run. It does not look much upon paper, but it was over a beautiful line of country, and the hounds, after the first mile, ran very fast. The only bit of plough I remember was between Chearsley and Chilton, coming back. In going to Chearsley we ran to the north of Chilton village, and coming back to the south. It is so long ago I can hardly remember who was out, but I remember Jack Thompson was at the corner of Chearsley cover when I got there; and I remember one of the Parkers—Algy, I think—giving the field a lead over a rail under Waterperry in the first part of the run. Frank Davenport was always there or thereabouts, going slow at his fences, till he retired to Mexico. Frank Gale, Fred Turrill, and the four

Castles, made up the hard riding division of the farmers.
Mr. Herbert Parsons, Colonel Ruck Keene, and Willy
Ashhurst, were out that day. Lord Macclesfield was
hunting the hounds as usual; Garsden, kennel huntsman and first whip; Charley Shepherd (the present
kennel huntsman), second whip.

Garsden always seemed to take it rather easily in the
field, and Lord Macclesfield and Charley did the most of
the work. But I remember one day, when his lordship
was out in 1872, Garsden and Charley, with Jack Thompson as field manager, did just about push them along.
I had then a pupil not all there, who wanted careful
handling, and who sometimes would do nothing, and
you could make do nothing. He was in one of those
fits that morning, so I put my man in a chair in the
hall to look after him, he being up in his room, and got
on my horse. I just caught the hounds going away
from Hell Copse. There were three couple running
another fox, which I foolishly tried to stop; for I have
found by experience it is not much good for a stranger
to try and stop hounds by himself. The hounds ran
through Horton Wood, and came away by Bechley for
the top of Stow Wood (where I caught them), then by
Barton village, under Headington, and ran to ground
under Shotover, after rising the hill—Jack Thompson
and Frank Davenport well to the fore all the time. We
did not wait a moment after he had gone to ground,
·but went straight back to the quarters where we had
left the three couple; found them still running; got
away at the corner of Shabbington Wood, through Oakley village, under Brill, and killed him in the open
under Dorton. I got a bad start again from Shabbington Wood, and did not know they were away till I saw
Garsden's grey horse going away three fields off, and
had to ride to catch them; but as luck had it I was in

at the death, the hounds turning in my favour, and saw them catch him in a hedgerow, along with Charlie, Garsden, Jack Thompson, and Frank Davenport. It was a capital day's sport How Jack did ride and bustle along that day. My horse was nearly beat.

May I say a word about parsons hunting? A man has no right to neglect his parish, or run into debt, but if he can hunt without doing either of these things, I cannot see the harm. Since I married I have, for pecuniary reasons, given up hunting, but I am quite sure of this, that neither my pupils or my parish are so well looked after as when I hunted. I lack energy. Hunting does put such life into you. The energy that you have to use in hunting seems to pervade all your other work. My dear father, H. O. Coxe, Bodley's librarian, and rector of Wytham, always had a few half-days every season, and no man ever worked harder or was more loved in his generation. I cannot think it wrong. I do think it wrong to run into debt, and, therefore, I find an oak walking-stick cheaper to keep than a hunter, and the bootmaker's bill less than the blacksmith's.

HILGROVE COXE,

Jan. 28th, 1884.

THE OLD HOUND.

My brave old hound, my bonny old hound,
   Here's a health, here's a health to thee!
And as years roll round mayest thou still be found
   Alongside in the chase with me.
Many's the day we have hunted away,
   And many's the track we have set;
And now I am told that thou art grown old—
   But there's life in the old Hound yet.

How oft has thy voice made the hunters rejoice,
  When its deep mellow notes were heard,
For well did they know that thy startled foe
  Must go his best pace on the sward.
Thou hast followed the chase with untiring pace
  From morn till the sun has set;
Thou hast lain at my feet when thy heart scarcely beat—
  But there's life in the old Hound yet.

Once did I think, when on the steep brink
  Of a dark shining rock thou stood,
That thy race was run, that thy life was done,
  As thou leaped o'er the yawning flood:
When thou fell on the rocks with the beaten fox
  I thought a hard fate thou hadst met,
But we found thee below with thy conquered foe—
  Aye! and life in the old Hound yet!

Thy coat is now grey, and thy strength doth decay,
  But thy heart is as brave and as true
As when first we went forth on the hills in the north
  In pursuit of the fleet-footed crew.
Men are to be found who would kill the old Hound,
  And his long years of service forget;
But a hand I'll ne'er lend to destroy my old friend,
  While there's life in the old Hound yet.

———

There's many a lass I have loved is dead,
  And many a friend grown old,
And unless with thee to the woodlands led
  This weary heart grows cold.
But as o'er hill and dale I fly,
  With thy voice to madden my brain,
All, all's forgot as to thee I cry,
  "Yoicks! have at him, old Hound, again!"

From LORD FERRERS.

THE DAYS WHEN I RODE WITH THE QUORN.

O ! bright are the fancies, and sweet the regrets,
    That arise at the sound of the horn ;
The friends of my youth, and the years of my fun,
    The days when I rode with the Quorn.

When I cantered away on the quickest of hacks
    To Six Hills so late in the morn,
And hunted unwearied o'er pasture and plough,
    What sport we had then with the Quorn !

What stories were told of the deeds of Tom Smith,
    Of the time ere Lord Stamford was born ;
We talked of Sir Richard, and followed the Earl,
    In the days when I rode with the Quorn.

How Treadwell would gloat o'er an oxer or brook ;
    We, boy-like, the obstacles scorn ;
How we fell and got up, and were never the worse,
    In the days when I rode with the Quorn.

Were the horses then really so stout and so good ?
    The covers of thicker blackthorn ?
The hounds truer-tongued, and the foxes more straight,
    In the days when I rode with the Quorn ?

And when we came back into Melton at night,
    Tired, happy, and draggled, and torn,
Were the ladies then really more lovely and kind
    Than those who now ride with the Quorn ?

Ah! youth, make the most of your day while it lasts—
  No sunset can equal the dawn!
I'd barter ten years of a peaceable life
  For a day when I rode with the Quorn!

"OLD SPORTSMAN,"
In Baily's Magazine, March, 1884.

A FRAGMENT.

Though the life-blood of Beauty with terror may curdle
  While brooding o'er risks which the sportsman must
    run,
Now imagines him lying in state on a hurdle,
  And turns but with sighs from the trophies he's won;
Yet, when England at tyrants would level defiance,
  Say what makes her sons so undauntedly bleed?
'Tis the chase—'tis the study of this noble science
  Gives spirit, and vigour, and health to the breed.

VARVICENSIS.

THOUGHTS ON HUNTING.

BY AN OLD HOUND.

IT is some years now since Mills wrote the "Life of a Foxhound," no doubt from authentic sources, and gave to the outer world some of those thoughts, feelings, and instincts which are freely passed to and fro within the kennel walls, though they seldom reach the world beyond. Times have changed since then; and it may not be uninteresting to those who would aspire to the name of sportsmen to know what we, who are certainly the parties most interested in the chase, think of the changes which have been introduced. Being somewhat young and inexperienced myself, I will not presume to give my own ideas on the subject, but faithfully record a conversation I had with a wise old hound who had seen many countries, during one of the hot days of the past month. He had come to our kennel, situated in a rare sporting but somewhat rural country, as Nimrod would have termed it, the autumn before, from the grass, for which I have my own suspicions he was getting rather slow, although he never would own to it, and consequently was looked up to with respect, and treated as an authority by all of us—an honour he well deserved, not only on account of his high lineage, but also for his really excellent qualities; for once or twice during the preceding season he had set us right when our fox was nearly lost, and been the means of killing him.

Our huntsman, as was his wont, had walked out with us in the park, and allowed us an hour of' thorough enjoyment, rolling in the short crisp turf, or stretched under the shade of the stately elms; when, seeing old Rallywood was not disposed for his usual nap, I ventured to ask if he did not think hunting in our land of ploughs and big woods a very tame affair in comparison with what he had been accustomed to on the grass.

"Why, no, youngster," was his reply; "though, I tell you, I did not much like the thought of exchanging N—— for D——shire, and quite intended the first day I was taken out to give the lot the slip, and make the best of my way back to my old kennels. I was so pleased with the fun (you remember it was a rare scenting day) and the sportsmanlike behaviour of

master, huntsman, and field, that I determined to stop
and have a little more of it, and, as you see, here I am
still."

"But it must be much better fun running over the
grass than toiling along, all mud and wet, in our greasy
fallows, often with not scent enough to enable' you to
hold the line?"

"You are quite right there; and on some days, when
there is nothing to interfere with us, the sport is
glorious. I remember one day in particular, when we
slipped away from every one, in a dense fog that suddenly came over, and killed our fox after forty minutes
without a check or crossing a yard of plough; but then
such a thing may not happen once in hounds' lifetime, and
as a rule after cub-hunting is over, we seldom have any
real fun—at least such is my experience. I like to hunt,
and nothing disgusts me more than having to gallop
about after the huntsman's horse, without being allowed
to put my nose down, and the constant danger of being
half laid open by the whipper-in's thong if I try to do
so. However, I never let that hinder me. And once
having slipped through a big ox-fence out of the way,
that young Jack was afraid to charge after me, I hit off
the line, and, with two couple and a half more that
came to me, had a good three-quarters of an hour, and
pulled down our fox, while Will, the huntsman, was
galloping and halloaing right in the opposite direction,
and, after having ridden his horse nearly to a standstill,
blew his horn at a rabbit burrow, and swore the fox he
had lost six miles back was gone to ground. Not that
Will is a bad fellow, and I believe he would like to see
us hunt; but then he is vain of his riding, and, as it is
the fashion for all the swells to ride at him and try to
cut him down, he soon loses his head, and thinks more

of his horse than his hounds. On one occasion both he and his field lost the pack entirely through jealousy, and were staring about on the top of a hill to know where we were gone; at the time we were quietly eating our fox in a hollow a mile behind them. Then the men who come out on the grass are, many of them, a great nuisance, and often have I been prevented making a hit by fifty or sixty pounding up a green lane, and then, seeing they had got too forward, pulling up in the very spot the fox had crossed. In fact, I hardly know which are the most tiresome to hounds, the hard riders or the shirkers; for one party drives them over the scent, and the other cuts them off and foils it. Again, the danger to hounds in the grass countries is not to be lightly estimated; and if you think that one half the field would alter their line at a fence because a hound was in the way, you are very much mistaken. Then, half of them are not so particular about the horses they ride as every one who hunts ought to be, and I, in my first season, was left for dead from a kick received from a celebrated grey. Kick hounds or horses either he would if he had the chance, and no doubt you will wonder why his owner, who was really a good sportsman, continued to ride him; but he was the best water-jumper in the hunt. I do not say, mind you, that there are not first-rate sportsmen, and many of them, in the shires—in fact, you would find more good sportsmen at a meet there than anywhere; but they are so largely leavened with those who are not sportsmen—men who go out because it's the fashion—men who go out to show their horses, or their boots, or to ride against each other—that it becomes, in the regular season, anything but a paradise for hounds.

"Why, I once knew a man gallop and halloa like a maniac, to get us on to a fresh fox that jumped up from

a hedgerow where our hunted one had turned short,
although anyone half asleep might have seen the difference in them; and thus he got up the heads of my
companions, and lost us our reward of blood, which was
nearly earned after a cold hunting run of over an hour-
and-a-half. Then I had a fellow throw down the end
of a stinking cigar just as I was feathering on the line
past him up a lane, and the vile smell so affected me,
that I could not hunt a yard for the rest of the day.
I believe I could have killed our fox had it not been for
him. Another—and, I believe, he wrote as an authority
on hunting—said that my poor old sister Reckless ought to
be hung when she got home, because she stuck persistently
to the line of her hunted fox when all the rest had given it
up, and he wanted to go and find another. However,
as I told you before, there are real good men who
understand us, our instincts, and our ways; such, for
instance, as M—— or T——, but they want elbow-
room on the grass. Now, here you have small fields,
and, as far as I can see, every man who goes to meet
hounds is a sportsman. Our huntsman, it is true, does
not ride so hard as Will, and I have seen him get off
at a big bank, or make for a gate, when a little more
quickness on his part, and the sound of the horn on *the
right spot, at the right moment,* would have put us on
better terms with our fox (for he never deceives
us, and when he does tootle, it is always a saving
of time to fly to the sound at once); but then
these are sins of omission, and he never loses
a fox for us by unnecessary interference. Then,
look at our master; his object is neither to jump
the biggest fences or race for twenty minutes; but he
likes to see his fox well found, well hunted, and
handsomely killed. He knows where and how to draw

so as to give us the best chance of finding; and if you hear his horn or holloa, you may swear it is gospel. And, as you know, last season, Tom, the second whip, was sacked, at a few minutes' notice, for punishing a hound unnecessarily, and when it was plain that the hound was right and the man wrong. No, no, youngster, you be contented here; the grass must have been a perfect elysium for hounds in the old days, when Meynell hunted from the borders of the Pytchley to Nottingham, and fields were small, and composed of only sportsmen; but the day is gone, the shires are the fashion, and a reasonable hound, who knows what sport is and hunting ought to be, is better out of a fashionable crowd than in it.

"Then, look at your country here : plenty of heath, which carries a scent second only—if second at all—to grass; no game to distract the attention of the young ones, and cause them to 'eat stick' before they really know what to hunt, chase, and avoid; and, above all, those magnificent hills and gulleys, which form no impediment to us, but stop those brutes of horses, whose greatest enjoyment, I firmly believe, is to gallop our sterns off. Think of the glorious bursts we have 'all alone,' while they are toiling and straining under their burdens up the miry, slippery hill-sides, and be thankful that there is no chance of your having a broken back because A—— has determined to be through that bullfinch before B——. Then, besides our master, huntsmen, and whips, all of whom are heart and soul in hunting, and think more of our work than their horses' fencing, have we not that glorious old parson J. R. to help us out of a dead lift when no one else is handy? and no man in England knows better how to do it. Now, youngster, don't ask any more questions, for I am sleepy."

N.

THE HILL'S WOOD RUN WITH THE BERKELEY HOUNDS,

25TH OF JANUARY, 1864.

Have you heard of the run with the fam'd Berkeley pack?
Of all our good things you'll admit 'twas the crack.
Our meet was at Kineton, and Thornbury Park
Held a fox who meant going, if need be, till dark;
And crossing the grounds, in his enemies' view,
For twenty-five minutes straight onward he flew.
The Colonel (1) rides first down a bank wide and steep
On "Charcoal" (who doesn't mean going to sleep);
Next the Huntsman,(2) whose cap is knock'd off and
    nigh stamp'd on—
Never mind, we are sailing away for Rockhampton.
Very few get a start, but, whoever they be,
Their number soon after increases by three:—
Three Nimrods, who late at their breakfast did tarry,
Got a "Nick" that conducted them straight to "Old
    Harry!"
For this fox we however now failed in our search—
P'r'aps a sanctum he found in the woods of the church.(3)
Now return'd from the Severn all ready we stood,
While the pack is preparing to rattle Hill's Wood.
Hark, a crash! they're away! thro' the park is his line—
A fair start, and no favour for your horse or mine;
Thro' Stone's verdant meadows right onwards we sail,
Those meadows describ'd as the Cream of the Vale.
On to Tortworth we press'd him without hesitation,
And follow'd our fox thro' the belt of plantation;

---

1. Colonel Berkeley, now Lord Fitzhardinge.
2. The huntsman, Harry Ayris.
3. Church Wood, a covert near Rockhampton.

But Tortworth's home coverts he gallantly spurns,
And ere we could reach him for Charfield he turns,
Cross the railway, and brook where most of the field
Still faintly pursuing, are destin'd to yield;
Then forwards to Ozleworth's coverts he bore,
Where the hunting continues, tho' riding is o'er;
Like leeches on flesh did the blood-thirsty pack
Up to Alderley hunt him, from Alderley, back;
Till near Wotton's old town, brave reynard dead beaten,
Ran to ground in a drain, was dug out, and eaten—
And now, who went best? Time fails me to tell
The separate deeds of each man that went well.
We had all (as the classics observe) "quantum suff,"
Or in English, our horses had had quite enough.
For the fences were tall and the lawyers not short,
But one lawyer (4) disposed of them all (out of court);
For leaving the merits of blood in abeyance,
This lawyer possess'd a trustworthy conveyance.
I shall ever remember that huge equine figure—
May his shade ne'er grow less (it can never grow bigger).
No ladies enlivened the scene with their faces,
Which perhaps may account for the absence of " Graces;"
But a skirter from Hill's wood beholding us, said,
" Why, surely some Miles's (5) are some miles ahead !"
Tho' the Banker,(6) on " All Fours," exclaimed," What
     a pity
These banks are not solid like those in the city;
For tho' clever my horse is considered, by heavens
At one time ' All Fours ' was ' all sixes and sevens.' "
Brave Charcoal (7) fell lame before reaching the goal,
But a Colonel (8) was there from a neighbouring Knole,

---

4. Edward Burges, Esq.
5. P. W. S. Miles, W. H. Miles, and R. H. Miles, Esqs.
6. W. H. Miles, on " All Fours," a favourite hunter.
7. " Charcoal," a favourite hunter of Colonel Berkeley's.
8. Colonel William, master of Knole Park.

And you'll understand what I mean if I say,
That he rode in his usual masterly way;
While we all must admit, that in quest of sly reynard,
There's no one rides straighter or lighter than Lennard.(9)
Then "a health to the pack" must conclude this long
    letter,
For where is the country can show us a better?
Where lives there an owner more popular? where is
The huntsman to vie with the bold Harry Ayris?
Long may Berkeley's wide coverts re-echo his voice,
And many such fox bid his old heart rejoice!
And oft may he talk of the run from Hill's Wood,
Till the day when he shows us another as good.
That you, reader, and I may be there on that day,
Is the prayer of the man (10) on the thoro' bred grey.

P. K. B. OLIPHANT.

ON THE DEATH OF THE FOX AT GOPSALL,

1868.

Not a halloa was heard, nor a blast of the horn,
    As away thro' the cover he scurried;
Not a bay from a hound, nor a who whoop was borne
    O'er the grave where poor reynard we buried.

We buried him silently, holding our breath—
    To sportsmen in future a warning;
But murder will out, and his untimely death
    Was known everywhere in the morning.

9. T. Lennard, Esq., of Bristol.
10. P. Kington Oliphant, Esq., (the author of the poem.)

His skin was unrent, his bones were unbroke;
  We laid him down just where he fell.
None at first had the spirit to venture a joke,
  Or laugh at so awful a sell.

Not loud but deep were the curses we said,
  And our hearts were o'ercome with sorrow,
As we thought on the fox that before us lay dead,
  And our hunt that was lost on the morrow.

We thought as we smoothed down his narrow bed,
  And arranged each muscular limb,
That the horn of the huntsman might sound o'er his head,
  But never in honour of him.

Loudly they'll talk of the deed that's been done,
  And Appleby's * squire much abuse;
And the people all round will be poking their fun,
  As soon as they get at the news.

But scarcely our mournful task was done,
  And we thought of resuming our firing,
When the vulpecide vowed he would give up his gun,
  And homewards talked of retiring.

Slowly he left, amid many a sneer,
  The field of his fame fresh and gory;
Tho' offered the brush, he declined with a tear,
  Such a basely-earned trophy of glory.

MORAL.

All ye who chance to read these lines,
  This moral may espy:
If with old gentlemen you shoot,
  Take care to wipe their eye.

Old George Moore, of Appleby, shot a fox accidentally.

FROM COL. J. ANSTRUTHER THOMSON.

---

*George Moore, of Appleby.

THE STABLE BOY.

Cima Rosa! Vallombrosa! Citron groves, sir?
　　Songs! Vines! Joy!
Grander far is High Leicestershire
　　To the heart of a Stable Boy.

I rise at dawn, nor feel forlorn,
　　But whistle for cheerful joy;
I look on all other pursuits with scorn,
　　Because I'm a Stable Boy.

All people that on earth do dwell
　　Hunt fallacies that cloy:
Oh! let them learn the way to do well
　　Is to copy the Stable Boy.

Drop ostentation and fiddle de dee,
　　Drop worries that annoy,
And set you down at the Coplow, free
　　Like a true born Stable Boy.

Pictures, and gems, and bric-a-brac stuff,
　　And every other toy—
Sell all, and buy a clean thoro' bred horse,
　　For so would a Stable Boy.

Thomson and Tailby could sweat their brow
　　In zeal for others' joy,
And toiled as hard for the Midland sport
　　As ever a Stable Boy.

SENT ANONYMOUSLY FROM MARKET HARBOROUGH
　　　TO COL. J. ANSTRUTHER THOMSON, NOV., 1880.

ES WRITTEN BY GEORGE TEMPLER, OF STOVER, ON
HIS GIVING UP THE SOUTH DEVON HOUNDS.

"MY OLD HORN."

Tho' toil hath somewhat worn thy frame,
   And time hath marred thy beauty,
Come forth, loved relic of my fame,
   Thou well hast done thy duty.

Time was when other tongues would praise
   Thy wavering notes of pleasure,
Now miser-like alone I gaze
   On thee, a useless treasure.

Some hearts may prize thy music still,
   But oh! how changed the story
Since first Devonia felt the thrill
   That roused her sporting glory.

Grace still in every vale abounds,
   But one dear charm is wanting;
No more I hear my gallant hounds
   In chorus blithely chaunting.

And there my steed hath found a rest
   Beneath the mountain heather,
That oft, like comrades sworn, we've prest
   In pleasure's train together.

And some, who at thy call would wake,
   Hath friendship long been weeping;
A shriller note than mine must wake
   Their deep and dreamless sleeping.

I, too, the fading wreath resign,
   For friends and fame are fleeting,
Around his * bolder brow to twine
   Where younger blood is beating.

Henceforth be mute, my treasured horn,
   Since time hath marred thy beauty,
And I, like thee, by toil am worn:
   Thou well hast done thy duty.

"ROUSE, BOYS, ROUSE."

Rouse, boys, rouse, 'tis a fine hunting morning;
Rouse, boys, rouse, and prepare for the chase;
Let not the time fly that's spent in adorning,
But on to cover hie at a good pace.
   There when you find, sir,
   The country's divine, sir,
The fences are whackers, the brooks are not small;
   But were they larger, sir,
   Boldly we'd charge 'em, sir,
Nor care a farthing, sir, how oft we fall.

Now from the fox he is driven, sir:
Hark how the valleys re-echo the call;
'Tis Osbaldeston's (1) voice reaching the heavens, boys,
Hallooing "forrard" loud as he can bawl.
   Then there's such spluttering,
   Spurting and sputtering,
Each one so anxious to be in the van;
   At the first rattling leap,
   Ox-fence or field of deep,
Onward the good ones creep—catch them who can.

---

*The late Sir Walter Carew, of Haccombe, Devonshire.
1. G. Osbaldeston, the celebrated "Squire."

White (2) on the "Wright," sir, is in the first flight, sir,
And quite out of sight, sir, of those in the rear;
And with him goes Neville, and Berkeley, (3) that devil
Who of good or evil knows no hope or fear.
    Molyneux strives at
    What horse scarce dare rise at,
Bold Plymouth (4) bullfinches close at his side;
    Musgrave (5) on Antelope,
    Baird (6) upon Jenny Hope,
Over the grassy slope forward they ride.

Coke (7) on the pony, sir, scarce has a crony, sir,
Standish has distanced the crowd very far;
Whilst at a place, sir, that few men dare face, sir,
Without checking pace, sir, drives Valentine Maher. (8)
Prince of the heavy-weights, Tweedale, (9) is bruising;
Maxse, (10) on Cognac, cannot be beat;
Poor Johnny Campbell's (11) horse long since refusing,
In struggling convulsion fits, dies at his feet.

---

2. "That well-known performer over a country or over a course, Mr. John White."
3. Sir Maurice Berkeley, afterwards Lord Fitzhardinge.
4. Lord Plymouth.
5. Sir James Musgrave.
6. Sir David Baird.
7. Mr. William Coke, of Norfolk, owner of "Advance."
8. Valentine Maher.—See Ante.
9. Lord Tweedale.
10. Mr. Maxse rode Cognac nine seasons.
11. Mr. Campbell, of Saddell. the author. He was riding a friend's horse, and the animal having unfortunately died, Mr. Campbell, hoping to conceal the disaster, begged the owner to put a price upon him, but the gentleman declining to do so, Mr. Campbell was obliged to reveal the calamity.

But our pace is the best, sir; the fox is hard prest, sir:
The hounds run with zest, sir, heads up and sterns
    down;
He can't reach yon cover; no, no, 'tis all over—
Hark how the death-pealing tallies resound.
    Dined—o'er our claret
    We'll talk of the merit
Of ev'ry choice spirit that rode in this run;
But here the crowd, sir, can be just as loud, sir,
As those who were foremost enjoying the fun.
Faster and faster they tell each disaster
Of bunglers and tumblers, and tailors who shun;
    While we drink round, sir,
    And drink to these hounds, sir,
Who over such ground, sir, could show us such fun.

ON THE DEATH OF CAPT. BERKELEY'S

(AFTERWARDS SIR MAURICE AND LORD FITZHARDINGE)

HORSE.

He turned to take a last long look, the evening sky was
    red,
The leading hounds already must have been two fields
    ahead,
Their fox was sinking rapidly, the chase was nearly done,
And he had gone the best, the first, throughout that
    glorious run;
And then in sadness down he looked to where beside
    him lay
The steed who'd borne his lord so well through all that
    wondrous day!

That morn he bounded fresh and fair, but now with
    stony eye,
With nostril stretch'd, and heaving flank, he'd lain him
    down to die!
'Twill soon be o'er, just one short neigh, a quiver and a
    groan,
His eye was set, his heart was full, 'twas thus he made
    his moan:

And is it come to this at last, my own my gallant steed?
Although I see, I scarce believe that thou art dead
    indeed.
And can it be that thou and I no more shall lead the
    burst?
No more cut down the customers, the fastest and the
    first?
No more shall fly the biggest fence that thins the horse-
    men's ranks?
No more shall charge the widest brook, though brimming
    to its banks?
Oft, oft, for many a rapturous mile, throughout the live-
    long day,
O'er many a field, o'er many a fence, we two have sailed
    away!
And now it almost breaks my heart to see thee lying
    there,
To know I cannot help thee with my fondest, tenderest
    care!
To feel that all is over, that thy bright career is past,
That spite thy form, and spite thy fame, this field has
    been thy last!

I bought thee as a yearling, and the promise of thy youth
For stoutness, speed, and gentleness, was well fulfilled
in truth.
Right worthy of thy line, thy sire, whom o'er the
Beacon Course
Newmarket well remembers as a good and honest horse;
Thy dam, whom legs and bookmakers all voted was a
hoax
Until at Epsom she came out, the winner of the Oaks.
And all their qualities were thine, unlike each meaner
steed
There was the pride of conscious power, the ease of
conscious speed;
Like them thou did'st not fret and chafe before hounds
went away,
But when the pace became severe, how far behind were
they!

Though high and strong the rails, on thee I needed not
to crane;
Though wide and deep the ditch might be, for thee it
gaped in vain!
When horse and man were going down, though good
and stout they were;
As if thy very feet were winged, thou'st borne me safe
and fair!
When hounds were racing for their fox, fast running
into view,
Still was thy mettle high and keen, still was thine action
true.
Foxes may fly and hounds may run, and horses still will
tire,
Yet 'twas not so with thee, my steed, thou wast indeed
a flyer!

From Tilton Wood to Loddington the hills are won-
    drous steep,
The vale of Belvoir, too, we know, will oft ride
    wondrous deep;
Fences are strong at Skeffington, and Belton seldom fails
To give account of sobbing sides, lost shoes, and quiver-
    ing tails.
From Barkby Holt to Stapleford, from Owston Wood
    to Glen,
I'll think of many a glorious run we ne'er can see again.
I'll think how many a hunting morn I've mounted thee
    in pride,
How many a dark December night we've plodded side
    by side.
Seasons roll on, and years pass by, so life flits day by day,
And others, too, will bear me well, though thou art
    passed away.
There'll still be music in the hounds, and pleasure in
    the chase
When other limbs beneath me bound, and others fill
    thy place;
But often shall I think of thee, and oft regret in vain
The favourite one, whose like I ne'er can hope to ride
    again.

THE FOREMOST FLIGHT.

I am a jovial sportsman, as every man should be,
A hunting life and a country life is just the life for me.
Our horses and our hounds are such no other clime
    can show,
For 'tis their delight, in the foremost flight, with a
    flying fox to go.

We are such plucky fellows we never fear a fall,
But boldly face the fence or gate, the spreading brook,
    and wall;
And those who crane or ride the lanes we hold are shy
    and slow,
And will ne'er delight in the foremost flight like birds
    with us to go.

And when we greet the well-known meet we quickly
    leave our hack,
And jump upon our hunter who is waiting with the
    pack.
Then crash into the cover both hounds and huntsmen go.
            [Line omitted.]

Hark there! I hear a challenge; it is old Music's note!
A chorus joins—what joyous sounds now in the breezes
    float.
"Hark! halloa!" cries the whip, for he has heard the
    huntsman blow—
The scent is good, and thro' the wood, by Jove! how
    they do go.

The huntsman cries, "Now, gently, pray hold hard, for
    there he breaks,
And straight across the open now his line he boldly
    takes:
He's fairly gone, so now we'll give a rattling tally-ho;
And now we're right in the foremost flight, with a right
    good start to go."

And now for twenty minutes we have had a glorious
    burst—
The pace begins to tell on them who yet have gone the
    first.
A check—so now we'll take a pull, and let our horses
    blow,
And set them right in the foremost flight again like
    trumps to go.

" Hark, Ranter! hark!" the huntsman cries. They hit
    him off again—
A sheet would cover all the pack now racing o'er the
    plain.
A view! it is the hunted fox, I know by yonder crow,
For 'tis her delight in the foremost flight with a sink-
    ing fox to go.

To reach yon distant cover, now, in vain game reynard
    tries ;
Old Venom runs into him, and he gamely fighting dies.
" Who whoop !" now cries the huntsman, who late cried
    " tally ho !"
Oh ! 'tis pure delight, in the foremost flight, in a run
    like this to go.

" Here's fox-hunting and fox-hunters ! and may we
    never trace
The man within old England's shores who would put
    down the chase ;
For such a man at once I scan as British sportsman's foe,
Who still delight in the foremost flight like bricks and
    trumps to go."

From Colonel Anstruther Thomson.

PATRICK'S BEAR SLAYING.

A PARODY.

Sing we how the mighty hunter,
He, the very strong man, Patrick,
Went to Norway at all seasons,
Crossed the North Sea in all weathers;
Very sick was in the steamers,
Very cold was on the fjelds,
Very hot was in the valleys,
Very hungry, very dirty.
Sleeping in a reindeer skin bag,
Sliding down the slopes in snow-shoes,
Sitting in hay-houses filthy,
Eating of the flad-brod flabby,
Dancing with Norwegian Piges,
Talking to the drengs and bonders;
Walking, toiling, night and morning,
In the snow and in the sunshine
Of the great lone land of Norway,
Of that flea-infested clime.

Three long years the mighty hunter,
He, the very strong man, Patrick,
Went to Norway in this fashion,
Suffered all this pain and hardship,
Till his friends began to mock him,
Till the world began to jeer him,
Saying, "What a fool is Patrick!
Almost like an idjot seems he."

Why did Patrick all these strange things?
Why commit these wondrous follies,
Leaving home, and peace, and plenty,
Horses, hounds, and fields and woodlands,

Deer and pheasants, game and foxes,
Beef to eat and Southdown mutton,
All that any man could wish for?
Why? because the bear, the "Feld-Kong,"
He, the "gammel man," the "Bjorn,"
Wandered free upon the fjeld,
Laughing at the drengs and bonders,
Taking sheep, and cows, and piges;
Caring nothing for their shot guns,
For their shouts, and shrieks, and howlings;
Living as he did aforetime
In the days of song and saga,
King of all the beasts in Norway,
Fearing no man, royal "Feld-Kong."

This it was that Patrick pondered
Three long years in vain endeavour,
Face to face to meet the monster,
And with gun or rifle slay him.
So at last in Surendalen,
He, the gammel man, the Bjorn,
Killing lambs and biting tree-tops,
Came too near the mighty hunter,
Came too near the strong man, Patrick.
In a reindeer skin bag laid he,
On the fjeld two nights watched he,
Till at last the bear, unthinking,
Caring nought for dreng or bonder,
Came too near the wily Patrick—
Came and sat down chewing dead lamb,
Pawing up with joy the pieces
From the earth where he had laid them,
Till a shot, well aimed and steady,
Lowly laid the bear, the Bjorn;

Till his giant form rolled over,
And his red eyes glittered strangely,
And the hunting knife gleamed o'er him.
Ended were his wild adventures,
Ended all his thefts and murders,
And his gambolings ungainly.
Now his skin is Patrick's sofa,
And his head hangs up with honour
In the house where, sung in story,
All his feats will be remembered.

L. C. M., JULY, 1882.

IN MEMORIAM.

"GREAT HOPES:" FOALED 1854, DIED 1875.

Nay, reader, don't start at the title,
  'Tis of only a horse—nothing more;
Only one of the lower creation,
  Whose loss 'tis my lot to deplore.
"Only a horse! well, what matters?"
  Quoth Dives; "'tis done in a trice:
Draw a cheque—the best horse that e'er hunted
  Can always be bought at a price."

Ah! Dives, men envy your fortune,
  You are floating through life with the stream;
You have got twenty hunters at Melton,
  And the pride of the Park is your team;
But I want just to ask you a question,
  So kindly one moment attend:
Be it man, be it woman, or horse,
  Can you ever replace an old friend?

Such a friend as we owe now and then
  To the sympathies born of the chase;
Raising horse to the level of rider—
  Such a friend we can never replace.
The box that stands empty and chill
  May shelter as perfect a frame,
But 'twill always seem sacred to him—
  'Twill always be called by his name.

Chesnut coat, sloping shoulders, small head;
  Legs that feared neither spavin nor sprains;
A mudlark when going was deep,
  With the blood of Small Hopes in his veins.
When Andover landed the Derby
  The theme of my song first drew breath,
And, as good on the road as the grass,
  Hunted up to the day of his death.

He had gone with the Queen's, when Charles Davis
  With horn made the forest to ring;
He remembered the bay Pantaloon,
  Bestridden by bold Harry King.
Since the day of that clipper from Denham,
  How many good men have departed,
When to Willesdon we ran in the hour,
  And Harrow Boy first was uncarted.

Not unknown where the doubles of Blackmore
  Lay many a steed on his back;
He had followed Jack Russell from Catstock
  With Poltimore's wonderful pack.
How oft with old Sam and Sir Maurice
  O'er Berkeley's green pastures he strode,
Heard the cheer of the keen Harry Ayris,
  Best huntsman, I wot, that e'er rode.

But dearest of all recollections—
  Old days now recalled to my view—
Are those when we hunted together
  In the land of the Badminton Blue:
The days of John Bayly and Friller;
  (What tales of their prowess are told!)
The days of the Merchant and Robber;
  The day ere grey Beckford was foaled;

When the Unicorn stood by the Lion,
  And Little was there on Champagne;
When the Colonel was great on Blue Pill,
  And Clark swore by Saffron and Jane;
When Methuselah carried the Marquis
  Thro' the longest and hardest of days;
When Alderley's gallant old owner
  Rode the first of his wonderful greys.

Unwelcome, perhaps, to the fair ones,
  Is the tale of what seasons have flown,
Since they first donned the Badminton button,
  And the "goddesses" yet were unknown:
Lady Blanche was the rising Diana,
  And one figure remembered will be,
That skimmed o'er the country on "Sunbeam,"
  With Jack Savile in front on B. B.

"Woe worth," wrote Sir Walter, "the chase,"
  When he sung of the hunting that kills;
Woe worth forty minutes' full pace,
  From Allen Grove up to the hills.
'Twas my gallant old horse's last effort—
  'Twas a mixture of pleasure and pain,
In that gallop where Grace's "blaze chesnut"
  Jumped walls, and ne'er jumped them again.

Farewell, gentle reader! If you
   These tales of past sport can endorse,
I will wish you no better than this,
   That some day you may own such a horse.
His name is inscribed underneath;
   His years were one over a score;
He was faithful and noble till death;
   His like I shall ride nevermore.

From BAILY'S MAGAZINE.

A DAY WITH THE QUEEN'S HOUNDS,
FROM POLL HILL, FEB., 1843.

Here's a health to Frank Goodricke, (1) of Pytchley
   the pride;
Here's a health to gay Gardner, (2) fam'd Melton's chief
   crack;
Here's a health to the high-hearted sportsmen who ride
Over Cheshire's deep fields with Jack White's (3) gallant
   pack;

Here's a health to the Scarlett (4) that gloriously shines
In the front of each field, where crack hunting is seen;
But the toast that best honours a bumper of wine
Is "Success to the staghounds, and long live the Queen."

Twelve o'clock was the hour, the meet was Poll Hill—
Noble "Hampton" had long been reserved for that day;
Close at hand stood the hounds, all expectant and still,
And thick gathered round them the brave and the gay.

---

1. Sir Francis Holyoake Goodricke.   2. Lord Gardner.
3. Captain John White.   4. Sir James Scarlett.

There was Rosslyn, (5) the rough, with the kindest of
    hearts;
There was gallant young Cambridge, (6) the loved of the
    land;
And, as beauty from valour and worth never parts,
Fair Theobald rode at the Prince's right hand.

There was Makepeace, (7) the merry, and Worley, the
    neat,
Dicky Vyse, thro' the water that swims like a duck,
And blithe-hearted Seymour, (8) a sportsman complete,
Only somehow this season he is not in luck.

There was well-mounted Wankelyn, and hare-hunting
    Poole;
Little Harford was there, too, that thinks he can ride;
Honest James, a true sportsman, courageous and cool;
Long Cox, (9) and a hundred good fellows beside.

From Windsor, from Hounslow, came guardsmen at
    score,
Bright souls never dimm'd with the vapours of fear;
Lucas (10) and Ogilvie, Holmes and Balfour,
And Ricards, that thinks of himself no small beer.

Time's up! lay them on—off like lightning they fly!
Grasps his rein, grips his saddle each hard-riding man;
And loudly rings Davis's (11) voice thro' the sky,
"Now catch 'em, ride over my beauties, who can."

---

5. Lord Rosslyn, master of the buckhounds.
6. The present Duke of Cambridge.
7. A leading man with the Queen's.   8. "Neighbour Seymour."
9. The banker.
10. Lucas, and Life Guards; Ogilvie, ditto; Balfour, of Newton Don.
11. Davis, the Queen's huntsman.

Twenty minutes have passed—Harrow steeple is near—
And of the three hundred that met at Poll Hill,
Like a regiment that's broke by the foeman, I fear,
But thirty are left that can live the pace still.

In Ruislip's deep meadows some come to a stand;
By Pinner's high fences some find their course barr'd;
And a loud swearing rustic, with pitchfork in hand,
Has pounded fat Hawkins fast in a farm yard.

" My horse lacks condition "—" I've lost a fore shoe"—
" Our efforts to catch them are hopeless and vain ;"
" I really believe the best thing we can do
Is, in hopes of a check, to jog on in the lane."

Now Northolt, now Greenford, are left far behind;
Twyford Abbey we've reached in our glorious career.
Still unflagging in strength, still unfailing in wind,
Over hill, over dale flies the matchless old deer.

O Elmore! (12) O Anderson! how could ye say
Of the horses ye sold us the thing that was not?
Piccadilly's proud cattle are dying away,
And Uxendon's flyers drop down to a trot.

Macdonough, (13) and Mason, and Bardolph-nosed Bean—
Of steeplechase riders at first we had plenty.
'Tis one thing to go for ten minutes, I ween ;
'Tis another to go for two hours and twenty.

Stout Stanley, (14) bold Errington, gallant Southampton,
Clauricarde, the dashing, and Pembroke, the kind,
Over Harrow's deep meadows in chase of fleet Hampton—
'Tis the pace that has left the foxhunters behind.

---

12. Elmore and Anderson, horse dealers.
13. Celebrated steeplechase riders.   14. Celebrated riders to hounds.

'Tis done! the brave quarry is hous'd safe and sound,
Regent's Park to the long lasting chase puts an end;
And of all the rare runs with this pack so renowned,
A faster and finer one never was penned.

Fill, fill up your glasses; a toast I propose—
No heeltaps, no daylight, no shirking be seen;
"Here's a health to Lord Rosslyn, wherever he goes;
Here's success to the staghounds, and long live the
    Queen."

From COL. ANSTRUTHER THOMSON.

HUNTING IN DURHAM.

Old fighting Durham! stubborn border land!
Leagued with thy sister, fair Northumberland!
From thy time honour'd battlements we trace,
From blood to blood, an honour'd sportsman's race—
Thro' Grindon, Carlton, Hartburn, to Fox-hill,
The name of Lambton * is re-echoed still!

If I could live one hundred thousand years
Amid this vale of sorrow and of tears,
Dash from my brow each cankering thought and be
What once I was, in youth and jollity!
At all Fortuna's coldest, hardest knocks,
I'd sneer, if Hartburn Grange holds in her gorse a fox!

---

*The celebrated Ralph Lambton.

Still as a whisper! no d—d loud hollo!
Nor cursed clodpole roaring, Tallyho!
No, not one word! Now then, ye hunters fleet!
The hounds are on him like a winding sheet:
Ride o'er them ye who can! their dappled sides ride over,
Burnhope and Elton, straight for Oxeye cover!

For him the ox-eyed goddess hath no charm—
See, on the road the ruthless furies swarm
All in a patch! just look! nay, never wait—
Crash goes the top-bar of that ill-hung gate!
By Jove! they're on him, see old Venus strive—
Have at him, beauties! Rive his life out, rive.

G. M. Sutton.

THE LAMBTON HOUNDS.

A Song.

Tune—"Weave a Garland."

Tho' midnight her dark frowning mantle is spreading,
   Yet time flies unheeded where Bacchus resides;
Fill, fill then, your glasses, his power ne'er dreading,
   And drink to the hounds o'er which Lambton presides;
Tho' toast after toast with great glee has been given,
   The highest top-sparkling bumper decides
That, for stoutness, pace, beauty, on this side of heaven,
   Unrivalled the hounds o'er which Lambton presides!
      Then drink to the fox-hounds,
      Those high-mettled fox-hounds;
We'll drink to the hounds o'er which Lambton presides.

Let Uckerby boast of the feats of the Raby,
  And Ravenscar tell what the Hurworth have done,
But the wide-spreading pastures of Sadberge can swear to
  The brushes our fleet pack of fox-hounds have won :
Then that Sedgefield, our country, all countries outvies,
    sir,
  The highest top sparkling bumper decides,
That we've foxes can fly, sir, or sinking must die, sir,
    When pressed by the hounds o'er which Lambton
      presides !
        Then drink to the fox-hounds,
        Those high-mettled fox-hounds ;
We'll drink to the hounds o'er which Lambton presides.

Of their heart-bursting "flys" let the Leicestershire
    tell us,
  Their plains, their ox-fences, and that sort of stuff ;
But give me a day with the Sedgefield brave fellows,
  Where horses ne'er flinch, or men cry 'hold, enough ;'
While the blood of Old Cæsar our foxes can boast, sir,
  May Lambton their only dread enemy be ;
And the green waving whins of our covers my toast, sir—
  Oh! the hounds and the blood of old Lambton for me!
        Then drink to the foxhounds,
        Those high-mettled foxhounds ;
We'll drink to the hounds o'er which Lambton presides.

G. M. Sutton.

A FEW GOOD RUNS WITH FRANK GILLARD.
1871 to 1878.

February 15th.—Met at Croxton Park. A large field assembled, and his Grace the Duke of Rutland gave the order to draw Coston Covert; and no sooner were hounds put into it, than three or four foxes were afoot. One bolder than the rest quickly went away southwards; the pack was not long in getting away after him, and it soon became evident that there was a scent. Passing just to the left of Wymondham and Edmondthorpe, at a rattling pace, we bore round for Woodwell Head, which covert this good fox disdained to enter, leaving it to our right hand, and the pace continued first-rate. We were not long ere we reached Gunby Gorse, through it like a shot, and from this point we made as straight as we could go for Morkery Wood, no one going better than the Duke, though there were many more in the front rank. A few fields before reaching the North Road, the hounds were in the same field with their fox, and were gaining upon him so fast, that it looked fifty to one upon a kill then and there; and Custance, the jockey, made so certain of it, he asked me for the brush; and reynard might have heard the request, for he put on a spurt, and reached Morkery Wood in safety, in which scent was not quite so good, which enabled him to dodge about for forty or fifty minutes; and as there were fresh foxes seen, it was feared our run one would beat the hounds, but they stuck to him, eventually driving him out away past Mickley Wood to the east corner of Witham Wood. Instead of entering it, this cunning old customer ran along just on the outside until reaching the south corner, and away over the North Road by N. Witham, after which we were brought

to slow hunting; but with great perseverance on the
part of the hounds, we reached Gunby Warren, where
we killed this stout fox, after running upwards of three
hours.

January 26th, 1872.—Met at Haverholme Priory.
An excellent day's sport—two good runs, both ending
with blood. The first run commenced from Eveden
Wood, ending at Swarby. This was a splendid gallop,
in which Sir Thomas Whichcote certainly had the best
of it. He was in front of a hard-riding field most of
the way, and, with but few, saw the pack run into their
fox. Time, forty-seven minutes; distance, from point
to point, six miles—much further the way hounds ran.
Second gallop started from Osbournby Hill Top. Ran
to Aswarby Thorns, then in a backward direction as far
as Aswarby Park; from thence straight away by Silk
Willoughby and Quarrington to Rauceby, when our
fox ran right away back on his foil to Aswarby Park,
and we killed him in the shrubbery by the gardens, thus
ending a fine day's sport. Time of this run, an hour
and twenty minutes. Sir Thomas Whichcote declared
it was the best day's sport he had seen for a great
number of years, and thought the first gallop the best
he had seen since Goosey's time.

January 14th, 1873.—Met at Bottesford. A fine
scenting day, which resulted in excellent sport. Our
first draw was Normanton little cover, and a fox being
at home, hounds were soon at work in good earnest;
but in spite of this, reynard stuck to his snug covert for
five minutes, when away he went to the left of Normanton village, after which he turned first one way and then
another, but all to no purpose, the pack was able to turn

equally quick and sharp. On nearly reaching the
Debdales, the fox found out it was no use twisting
about any longer, so he shot away to the right, crossing
the Nottingham and Grantham railway, and over the
river Devon, and straight for Scrimshaw's mill, when he
suddenly changed his course by turning sharp round
past Muston, leaving it away to the left, re-crossed the
river Devon, on to and through Shipman's plantation,
close past Breeder Hills, when our fox was viewed by
the field only a field ahead of the hounds, and they
were not long then in racing into him; caught him just
before reaching Woolsthorpe wharf, thus ending as fast
a gallop as I ever saw, lasting thirty-five minutes.
Hounds did not require the least assistance from beginning to the finish. As good a gallop as this was, it
proved only a pipe-opener for a fox, who was found at
Jericho, going straight away past Elton and Orston at
a pace quite fast enough over those ploughs for the
horses to keep with them. Getting on to the grass,
they raced on passed Thoroton, and forward to the
Coronation cover (Flintham), where we unfortunately
changed to a fresh fox, but scent being so good, and
our horses a bit pumped, nothing could be done to right
matters; all we could do was to keep pegging away; and
on reaching the Red Lodge, a turn took us by Screveton
and Scarrington to Whatton, when it became dark; and
with difficulty we succeeded in stopping hounds, thus
ending a real good and very hard day for both hounds
and horses. Mr. George Drummond was the only
gentleman to get to the end of this good run.

January 6th, 1875.—Met at Piper Hole. A fox
found at Clawson Thorns, did not give much sport; our
next was found at Harby Hills, and was run over the

vale to Hose Gorse and lost. Sherbrooke's gorse was then called upon, and it supplied us with a good stout fox, who went away over the Smite as bold as a lion, and getting a good start after him, hounds ran tremendously hard for forty-five minutes, without a check. The line which we ran was pretty straight as far as Widmerpool New Inn, being just to the left of Hickling, and over Hickling Standard, through Parson's Thorns without dwelling, and straight for the New Inn. Then he turned for Kinoulton Gorse, through it, and straight to and through Owthorpe Borders to the Main Earths (this was reached in the time above mentioned, viz., forty-five minutes, and out of a large field very few were to be seen with hounds, many coming to grief). Fortunately hounds were stopped, and reynard then made straight for Hoe Hill, but some boatmen on the canal prevented him from going into the covert, and, being only a field ahead, it seemed a certainty we should kill him directly; but this game fox struggled on field after field, to the left of Ratcliffe, and then for Cotgrave Gorse, and it being quite dark, we knew not what had happened, whether hounds killed their fox, or ran him to ground, but it was one or the other. We were afterwards informed many of the Melton horses were left out all night in the Widmerpool country.

April 12th, 1876.—Belvoir. Splendid finale to the season, on the Leicestershire side. Through a heavy snowstorm we failed to do any good with a fox which was found on Saltley Heath, but late in the afternoon we found a good one in Bescaby Oaks, who first of all took a turn over Croxton Park, when away he went past Sproxton Thorns and Coston Village to Coston Covert, and through it, without dwelling a moment. Up to this point the pace had not been very severe, though we always had to keep pegging away; but after getting clear of the last-named covert, hounds raced past Wymondham, then, bearing to the left, made for Woodwell Head, but no dwelling there. By the time we galloped to the south end, the pack was streaming away towards Cottesmore Gorse, just skirted it, and ran round by Teigh, and killed near Edmondthorpe, thus making a good finish to a capital run of something over two hours. Distance, as the crow flies, from Croxton Park to Cottesmore Gorse, is ten miles. Those whom I noticed to the end were Miss Miles, (who was on a visit at Belvoir Castle, and was riding a horse of his Grace's,) Captain Longstaffe, Mr. John Hardy, Mr. Turner Farley, Mr. James Hutchinson, Captain King, and the Rev. Mr. Mirehouse.

January 22nd, 1877.—Easton Hall. Found at Easton Wood, and ran a ring first of all round by Burton Sleights and Stoke Park Wood, turning back to where we found, and then changed to a fresh fox, who led us a nice dance, or rather gave us a splendid run. He went away much the same line as the first fox, but instead of entering Stoke Park Wood, he skirted it, and crossed over the railway, and away for Boothby—hounds running through like shots and away like a flock of pigeons for Humby Woods, passing just to the right of them. We rattled along and soon crossed the famous Lenton Brook, and leaving the village to our right, we ran for Keisby Wood, just running through the north corner, when we were fairly landed in the finest country in the Belvoir hunt, going as straight as we could go for Aslackby village. A field or so before reaching it we were in the same field with our fox, and it looked fifty

to one on a kill then and there, but unfortunately a large
flock of sheep were running between the fox and the
pack, which not only prevented a view, but the sheep
molested the hounds by running all amongst them,
which enabled the fox to reach Aslackby village, and the
natives then took up the chase as long as they could
view him. This circumstance bothered us more than
the flock of sheep, and some minutes were lost before
we recovered the line, and when we did, hounds could
never do much more good; still we hunted on by fits
and starts past Dowsby, and away over the Fen district
to within two miles of the Forty Foot. Distance, as
the crow flies, is not less than fourteen miles, and it is
impossible to run over a finer line of country.

March 17th, 1877.—Three Queens. The Heath
coverts all proved tenantless, but we found a good fox
at Buckminster, who made away over Saltby Heath,
thence by Wyville to Stoke Rochford Park, and from
thence away between Skillington and Woolsthorpe to
Gunby Warren, to ground. Some fields before reaching this covert, we several times viewed our fox just
ahead of the pack, and he was dead beaten. Just at
this critical moment a very dark cloud passed over us,
when there was not a particle of scent, which enabled
reynard to reach the earths in safety. The time of
this good sporting run was an hour and forty-five
minutes; distance, about fourteen miles. Lord Gran-
ville, Lord Wolverton, and Major Whyte-Melville were
out; the latter gentleman expressed himself to me as
being very pleased with the sport.

December 12th, 1877.—The House, Melton Mowbray. This day will be remembered as the "Pink

wedding day." His Grace arranged for the hounds to meet in honour of the marriage of Mr. Cecil Samuda and Miss Cecile Markham. The Duke of Rutland and members of the hunt went to church in hunting costume, and after the grand ceremony and breakfast were over, a very large field accompanied the pack to Burbidge's cover, where a fox was found, who proved quite equal to the occasion. A crowd of foot-hunters had stationed themselves on the high ground overlooking the cover, and bold reynard swam the river and ran through their very midst. Once clear of them he ran a bee line, with the hounds pretty close to his brush, away by Burton Lazars, Berry Gorse, Laxton's Spinney, crossed the Whissendine brook, and passed just to the right of the village, and from thence, forward nearly to Ranksboro' Gorse, then wheeled round, running by the Punch Bowl and Wheat Hill planting. Here there were two or three foxes, but the pack stuck to their game fox, who made his way back by Wild's Lodge and Burton, to ground, by the Dalby Road near Melton. Time, an hour and fifty-three minutes; a good sporting run.

March 6th, 1878.—Ash Wednesday. Met at Piper Hole. In a gale of wind we ran a fox from Holwell Mouth at a rattling pace, away over the vale, and passed to the right of Nether Broughton, and forward for some distance in a direct line for Hickling, when we wheeled round, running between the two Broughtons, and nearly reached Old Dalby, when a turn, right handed, took us over the hill; after which, we took a straight line for Willoughby-on-the-Wolds, killing our fox close to the village. Time, one hour after leaving Holwell Mouth.

On Ash Wednesday, 1867—From Clawson Thorns we ran over nearly the same line of country, and then killed close to Willoughby.

March 29th, 1878.—Met at Weaver's Lodge. For the first time this season his Grace hunted with his hounds on the Lincolnshire side of the country, and we were lucky enough to have a real good hunting run, which was quite unexpected through the very dry weather. There were no less than two and a half brace of foxes at Newton Woods, and, strange to say, the one I viewed away in front of the pack, I remarked, was our Hose Gorse fox, who had, during the season, given us three nice gallops from that cover, in the direction of Croxton Park; and it appears I was right, for he ran almost a straight line for Croxton Park, though he ran us out of scent between Wyville and Stoke Pasture. The line was away through Haydon's Southings, Ropsley Rise, Ponton Park wood, crossing the Great Northern Railway between the Pontons, and passing to the left of the school Plats to where he beat us. Distance, eleven miles as the crow flies.

————

F. GILLARD.

A SEASON'S SPORT WITH THE QUORN.

T o covert, brave sportsmen, on on, and away!
H ark! hark! to the cry of the hounds!
E ach one in his musical note seems to say:

Q uick! for'ard, my comrades! we mean it to-day,
U ntil the death holloa resounds!
O ne shake of his toilet, the bold, but the sly
R eynard takes up the cue, and he sails—
N ow to baffle and beat them his hardest he'll try.

H ave at him, my beauties, as onward we fly
O ver hedges and ditches and rails;
U p hill or down dale, through woodlands, o'er rill,
N o matter what comes in the line,
D o your best to be with 'em, your motto be still,
"S traight forward" to the ending of time!

The season of 1883-4 commenced on Monday, November 5th, at Kirby Gate, as usual. There was, as may be expected, a large field out, and many carriages and other vehicles well filled, all bent on seeing as much of the fun as possible. Fortune invariably favours the Kirby Gate meet, and this was no exception, for a good fox was found in Gartree Hill, who went away like wildfire, at a minute's notice, over the Burton flats, then round to the right by Leesthorpe, Wheathill spinney, and into the shrubberies at Little Dalby, where many of the sportsmen were left, this being such an awkward place to get away from on account of the wire fencing which runs around it. Hounds were quickly away, and hunted their fox beautifully back by Wheathills, Berry Gorse, and on past Whissendine, thence by Ashwell (having ran within a few fields of Ranksborough Gorse) to Teigh, where he was rolled over in among the cabbages in a cottage garden, after a really nice run of an hour and twenty minutes. Being a long way in the Cottesmore country, we had a good trot back for another draw. A sharp twenty minutes from Thorpe Trussells, ending the day close to Mr. Chaplin's house at Burrow Hills.

On Friday, November 16th.—Baggrave Hall. The first time of meeting here since the lamented death of poor General Burnaby. A leash of foxes were in the covert; hounds quickly killed one, and went away with another—being close at him, they ran, at an awful pace, a ring by Hungerton and back; then, passing the hall, took us over a nice line of country, by Thimble Hall, and, leaving Twyford on the right, crossed the brook (which brought the usual fun and grief), and then ran pretty direct to Thorpe Trussells, away without dwelling a second, and then, turning to the left hand, they ran through Ashby Pastures and Cream Gorse, the fox going to ground just beyond. Time, forty-five minutes.

Friday, 23rd.—Rearsby was the fixture. After a gallop in the morning to ground, we found as good a fox as ever ran in Barkby Holt, and such a scent did he leave, that hounds quickly ran away from almost every horse. He was a wonderful fine fox, and could be plainly seen now and then about a couple of fields ahead. Running to the right of South Croxton, he turned up to Baggrave, and, darting through the covert like a shot, he passed the hall, hounds racing as if they had him all the time in view, and everyone riding apparently for their very lives; in fact, I hardly ever remember seeing a field so determined and yet so quickly squandered. The beautiful grass valley by Car Bridge and Lowesby was crossed at a terrific pace, and when Springfield Hill was reached, a half-dozen horsemen alone were in sight. It is my belief that foxes were changed here, for there was a slight check on the railroad, down which I fancy our fox had gone, but a holloa just ahead took hounds to it, and, catching up the line, they ran past Tilton, thence by the Skeffington Vale and Whatborough Hill to the Cottesmore Woodlands, just before reaching which we found that a brace of foxes were in front, and both fresh ones, so this fine run ended without blood. Time altogether, about an hour, the first half being much the quickest.

Monday, 3rd December.—Six Hills. A nice gallop, from Ella's Gorse to ground in Shoby Scholes occupying the first part of the day; after which, we went to Thrussington Wolds; found at once, and had a charming fifty minutes, killing him in the open near Long Clawson; the line being first towards Six Hills, then sharp to the right towards Shoby and Lord Aylesford's covert, keeping both just on the right hand; and after pointing towards Grimstone, a turn to the left took us by Old Dalby Wood and Holwell Mouth, and up to the Clawson road, where our fox was headed and turned into the Vale—not, however, to travel far over it, for he was dead beat, and hounds getting a view quickly after, rent his jacket.

A very fine hunting run was brought off on Saturday, December 22nd, when the fixture was Costock. The meet itself was a small one, but late comers, including several ladies and gentlemen from Nottingham, made up a good-sized field ere a fox was found. Among those present, as far as I can now remember, were Mr. Coupland and Mr. Duncan Coupland, Miss Brooks (Whatton), General Chippendall, Mr. Wm. Paget, Mr. C. and Mr. A. Martin, Mr. J. D. Cradock, Capt. Fowke, Mr. and Miss Tidmas, Capt. O'Neal, Major Robertson, Mr. Cockrayne, Mr. G. Farnham, Captain Warner, Mr. H. and Mr. M. Lewis, of Nottingham, also Mr. John Robinson and his son, who went wonderfully well through the run, and saw almost as much of it as anyone.

Our fox was found in Bunney Old Wood, and went first towards Windmill Hill, but, being headed (and nearly killed) he turned back, and got clear away to the Intake Wood, then, without dwelling a second, made his point towards Wysall. Mr. Charles Martin, viewing him away, said, " what a very fine fox he was." Turning to the right from Wysall, hounds hunted him beautifully pretty direct to Prestwold, taking Wymeswold in the line. On getting to within a field of Hoton covert, a very short and peculiar turn was made (it being near here that Major Robertson, in jumping through a thorn fence, unfortunately got struck in the face, and lost an eye in consequence). The turn mentioned took us short back for two or three fields towards Ella's Gorse, then another turn to the right took us slowly on by Burton—scent at this time being bad, hounds had to keep their noses down to make it out until after passing Walton Thorns, Mr. Cradock's ash spinney, and reaching Mr. Coupland's farm at Six Hills. A brace of foxes were immediately after this in front of us, and it was impossible to tell whether we went on with the right one or not. Scent all at once improved, and the pace was really good for the next thirty minutes. Old Dalby being kept a field or two on the right hand, we pretty quickly reached Broughton station, near where the railroad was crossed, and hounds pointed for Curates Gorse. This latter covert was kept some little distance on the left, while the pack swept gaily on, with not more than two or three followers anywhere near. I may mention, the field began to tail the moment hounds increased the pace on Mr. Coupland's farm, and I never saw a whipper-in afterwards! After crossing the Broughton road, on the right of the Curate, hounds dipped into the valley, then, swinging round to the left, soon climbed the hill of Hickling Standard, and passed on the very edge of Parson's Thorns, but not a hound entered, the line being carried on towards Kinoulton Gorse; but about midway between the two they (the hounds) turned to the right, and the two villages of Hickling and Kinoulton were passed and left behind. Soon after this my hopes were raised very high, for I saw the fox, with his back up, not more than a field ahead, and not unnaturally the thought of a speedy termination, with a glorious kill in the open, at once crossed my mind; this, however, was not to be, although we kept close at him for some time yet to come. He having crossed the canal by the swing bridge, I was put off the line for a few valuable moments by two labouring men, who said they were quite sure he had not gone over; and, as another instance of how little notice should be taken of such people, the fox had crossed under their very feet, and they had not seen him. Immediately after this I got another view at him, crossing a stubble field, and luck was again against me, for Mr. Coupland, who would no doubt have been a great help, got a very nasty fall over a stile, and was prevented coming on for some little time. At the next road hounds again checked, the fox having ran down it for some distance, and some traffic being between him and the hounds, made it more difficult for them to own the line. Three or four fields further on, and the canal was again reached, at a very sharp turn which there is in it. Up to this the fox had ran, but, instead of swimming over, had turned short to the left along the towing path, on which he kept for perhaps a half-mile. Directly after leaving this, the Smite crossed our line, and, in addition to the brook itself, there was a fence on the landing side, which made it almost impossible to jump at that end of the day. Having a quick eye, Mr. A. Martin soon saw a place where the rail on the far bank could be broken, and the brook being narrowish just here, we landed over safely, and pounded along after hounds, who were running again very smartly now in the direction of Kaye Wood, and eventually passed it close by the keeper's house. Keeping a straight course we were not long in reaching Colston Bassett, where the fox had been seen two minutes before, and dead beaten; still he managed to struggle on, and at Langar darkness was coming on at such a pace that it was found impossible to continue the pursuit; and however richly hounds deserved their fox, they had to be stopped, and come home without him, after hunting him for three hours and forty minutes in the most persevering manner possible. Although the longest point would not be more than thirteen miles, the country crossed would not measure less than twenty-three, and this all grass, with the exception of ten or twelve fields, and one covert only touched, viz., Mr. Cradock's ash spinney, near Six Hills, near where it is most likely foxes were changed.

A short description may be given of a very long run which took place on Monday, Dec. 31st, when the meet was at Widmerpool New Inn. There was a good-sized field out, and the favourite covert, Curates Gorse, was the order, where we at once found. Going away by the meeting place, our fox then turned to the left, and ran parallel with the Fosse road as far as Willoughby, then bearing to the left, re-crossed it, and then steering for the Vale, he passed the Broughtons and Mr. Sherbrooke's covert; after which he bore round to the right, and ran up to the Wartnaby hills, and passing Little Belvoir and Holwell Mouth, got again into the vale by Clawson, from which another turn took us over the hills, this time to keep straight ahead. Having passed Grimstone Gorse and Lord Aylesford's covert, we kept on thence by Ragdale, and were soon afterwards treated to a sby at the Hoby raspers, at one of which Count Kinsky got an awful fall, a bottom which looked to be eighteen or twenty feet wide, with stake and bound fence on taking off side. He was picked up insensible, but soon came round, and joined hounds again after they had passed Cossington Gorse, and reached Seagrave village. Hounds threaded the village, and then pointed for Barrow-on-Soar, but, turning again to the right, crossed over by Pandy and Burton, got within a few fields of Wymeswold, and were stopped in the dark when nearing Old Dalby. About four gentlemen only got to the end of this run.

Friday, Jan. 11th.—Great Dalby was the meet, and after running a fox to ground at Leesthorpe, we found in Thorpe Trussells, and ran a cracker, the line being by Adams' Gorse, then over the beautiful and good-scenting old Burrow hill steeplechase course, thence to the left by Sir Francis Burdett's covert, Gartree Hill, over the Burton Flats to Burbage's covert, where we dwelt not a moment, but running straight through, hounds kept up the pace towards Stapleford Park, rolling their fox over handsomely when within three fields of it. Time, just over an hour.

Monday, 14th, was productive of another good run of about the same time, Six Hills being the meeting place. A slow hunt from Cossington Gorse was all that was done in the morning, when we went on to Thrussington New Covert, and found as fine a fox as is often seen. He went away by Six Hills, and then, turning to the right, got close up to Shoby Scholes, when another turn to the left took us over the Wartnaby road, and pointing in the direction of Wymeswold, from which he turned, and shortly after passed Old Dalby, thence on by Lord Aylesford's Covert and Shoby, worked back by Ragdale, where he was rolled over in the open. The following sketch will show that he must have been pretty stiff, for he stood up perfectly straight when dead, and without the slightest assistance.

Another fox was found in Walton Thorns, and killed in the open, in fifteen minutes; and another being halloa'd for'ard at the same time, gave us a remarkably pretty gallop, running by Wymeswold, Ella's Gorse, Willoughby, Wysall, and beat us at or near to Widmerpool just as darkness was coming on.

The thirty-two minutes which was so thoroughly enjoyed on the day after the Loughborough ball should, I think, be mentioned briefly.

Thursday, 17th Jan.—Prestwold, at 12. Of course there was a much larger field than is seen on this side on any ordinary occasion. Our first fox was found in Willoughby Gorse, and bowled over just before reaching Widmerpool. Time of this spurt, fifteen minutes.

All were pleased when the master now gave the order for Curates Gorse, which has been the starting point of so many good runs. A fox was quickly found, but on account of the number of people he could not get away so quickly as usual, and indeed he was nearly chopped, through being headed and turned back from the road, which was lined. Making his next attempt on the upper side, he got clear away, and nothing could be more lively than the run which followed. After pointing for Upper Broughton, he swung round to the left, crossed the road, and dipped at once into the valley—hounds racing and shooting through each succeeding fence like so many arrows. A turn to the right taking us under both the Broughtons, and the brook which crossed our path, had the effect of thinning the field most unmistakeably, one gentleman getting a fearful ducking, his horse walking about on the top of him while he was under water, and he eventually had to ride home to Leicester minus hat, whip, and one stirrup, while a dozen or fourteen others helped to fill its banks. Hounds in the meantime were racing away and waiting for no one, their line being by Mr. Sherbrooke's Covert, and pointing their heads in the direction of Kaye Wood; but again turning to the left, they wheeled round, and running beside the canal up to Hickling village, they were seen, fox and hounds, tumbling over and over down the embankment, when a real hearty whoo-hoop rent the air. Among others, Mr. L. Rolleston went remarkably well, and was one of the first to see the fox rolled over.

On the day following, viz., Friday, 18th, the fixture was Quenby Hall—and another grand day's sport was the result. The first fox was put up in the open by foot people, but he went to ground at Ingarsby, and we went on to Botany Bay. A traveller was quickly found, and, dashing through the Coplow, made at once "over the hills and far away." Passing by Tomlin's spinney, and climbing the next hill, the pace was too great for the horses, and hounds literally ran away from them. They ran at a tremendous pace, leaving Billesdon on the right, and Skeffington on the left, to Rolleston. Time up to this, twenty minutes. Scent now failed considerably, and the rest part was hunting, although at a fair pace. A lot of country was ran over by Keythorpe and East Norton, the fox being finally killed in the open near Loddington, in the Cottesmore country, after having ran through a good portion of Sir Bache Cunard's. This made the sixth fox killed in the open during the last four days.

On Friday, Jan. 25th, the meet was at Ashby Folville. A fox was found first in Thorpe Trussells, and hunted steadily by the Punch Bowl, Pickwell, and lost at Cold Overton, when we came back to Ashby Pastures, and found what had proved to be, on two previous occasions, the worst fox ever seen, for he ran the whole time like a very bad rabbit; and it is most surprising that such a fox could have behaved so badly, for he knew a great deal of country. He went away this time the same line as before, and was trying his twisting dodges, when he must have found this time it would not pay. Coming away beside the road towards Gaddesby, the pace was terrific as they skirted the end of that village, and swung round over the grasses by Ashby Folville. Another turn to the left took them up the hill, and, after running between the two coverts of Thorpe Trussells and the Pastures, they pointed for Kirby, but turned before reaching it, and taking in the line Gaudilope and Burton Lazars, after which hounds quickly entered Mr. Burbage's Covert. So far it had been capital, but was not yet over. As hounds were going in on one side, the fox was going out at the other, and coming back to the river, which saved us the trouble of crossing it. The line was now direct across the Burton Flats to Stapleford Park, which the fox reached not two minutes in front of hounds, and was immediately after bowled over handsomely. Time, an hour and five minutes; distance, as the crow flies, nine miles; as they ran, thirteen.

Monday, 4th Feb.—There were two charming gallops to ground. Meeting place, Widmerpool New Inn. The morning was spent in blank draws; but when Lord Aylesford's Covert was reached the proceedings considerably altered, for a very wide-awake fox was away before hounds entered the covert, and being clapped on to him without loss of time, the twenty minutes which followed was of the very best description: the line being round Grimstone, through the Gorse and Saxelby Wood, thence by Old Dalby, to Broughton station, to ground beside the line. Being a large pipe drain, there was no difficulty in bolting him; and after another nice run, he returned to the same drain, and was left in peace.

Monday, 11th.—A very wild morning, and unlike hunting. The fixture was Thrussington, and Cossington Gorse was first drawn. This covert produced a fox who went to ground at Ratcliffe-on-the-Wreak, beside the river, at a time when the most fearful storm of hail and rain was falling that is often one's lot to be out in. The day now cleared up nicely, and we went on to Thrussington Wolds for another fox—quickly finding; but scent was only very moderate until towards the end. Hounds hunted beautifully by Ragdale, thence by Shoby and Hoby, then to the left up to Grimstone, and on to Old Dalby, and down towards Broughton station; but, turning back, the line was carried over the Wartnaby hills and into Saxelby Wood, where they got on better terms with their fox: and now they began to run in real earnest, and the line of grass, too, was very pretty. Clean through Saxelby village they raced him, and at Asfordby bowled him over in a cottage garden, after a remarkably sporting run.

On Monday, March 10th.—Widmerpool New Inn was again the meet, and Curates Gorse again the first draw. A fox being quickly found, we were away almost in no time, and in eleven minutes afterwards were at the edge of Mr. Sherbrooke's Covert. I don't know the distance, but this seemed to me to be very quick work, and I took out my watch twice to be sure that I had not made a mistake. The fox being holloa'd on one field ahead, we ran by Hose brickyard and Clawson to the Thorns, thence to Piperhole Gorse, when hounds divided. Our horses were too much beat to be able to catch and stop either lot, so each went their own way: one lot running their fox to ground at Harby Hills, the others theirs to ground at Old Hills.

Saturday, 22nd March.—A day on the Forest, Charley Cross Roads being the meeting place. Some coverts were drawn blank in a line for the Whitwick Rocks, where we found, but our fox was killed almost immediately, which was a sad blow, as foxes on this side were well known to be very scarce. However, we had luck in store, for at the One Barrow Reservoir a very stout old gentleman was in waiting, and who kept us for the next two hours busily engaged ere he yielded up his life. Going first by the One Barrow

Farm, he ran a circle, and back to his starting point, thence to White Horse Wood and Sheepshed, and, instead of going on to Garendon, he turned to the left, and keeping Oakley and Piper Woods on the right hand, ran pretty straight to Belton, and then turned short to the left along the Water Meadows, where there was a capital scent, and which was a very pretty part of the run. This led us to Gracedieu Manor, hounds crossing the Park, and pointing for the Cadement Wood, but instead of entering it, they bore to the left, and crossing Sharpley Rocks, once more passed One Barrow. This was his last time, for our fox now put his head for a different line, and from which he was not again destined to return. Crossing by the Oaks Church and Hiveshead we soon reached Longcliffe, and passing on the right of the Privets, ran over Whittle Hill, and into the Out Woods; one turn round, and away by Caron's Piece, and on to Beacon Hill; and running through the Beacon Planting, hounds got a view just outside, and rolled him over, and so ended another capital day.

The above are, although feebly written, a slight example of the many excellent runs which have been enjoyed during this very famous season—certainly by far the best it has been my good fortune to have seen. It is an old saying that a good scent makes a good fox, and in the season just past, this may be said to have been fully illustrated, for scent has been better and foxes have run straighter than perhaps has been known for a very many years. I hope it may be as good next. Then with a good pack of hounds and a good stud of horses, and a prosperous season for the farmers, there will be lots of fun and enjoyment for those who think that, among the few things most worth living for, fox-hunting is one.

T. FIRR.

THE GALLANT LITTLE GREY.

I've got as good a little horse as ever you did see,
. So well he lifts his foreleg up, so nice he bends his knee ;
His action high, his quarters good, and such a depth of girt,
And a rattling pair of hocks and thighs to lift him
   through the dirt.
     My gallant little hunter,
     My dashing little grey !

Now see him at the covert side with snaffle bridle on,
While other horses chafe and fret, how quietly he'll
   stand ;
And when the hounds have found their fox, and settled
   to him steady,
He'll champ his bit and shake his head to show you he
   is ready.
     My gallant little hunter,
     My dashing little grey !

Five minutes more are over, there's a halloo "gone
   away !"
The scent is good, the pace first-rate, there is no time
   to stay :
The scent is good, and up yon hill I'll venture any bet
The cocktails will be sobbing, and the swells all in a fret
     At my gallant little hunter,
     My dashing little grey !

Now twenty minutes past and gone, the swells begin to
   crane
At a great high stile upon a bank, and a drop into a lane.
My little nag can stand and jump, which oft saves me a
   burst,
And now but two are with the hounds, and now, by
   Jove, I'm first
     On my dashing little hunter,
     My gallant little grey !

COLONEL THOMSON'S BEST RUN WITH THE ATHERSTONE,

1849.

JANUARY 1st, Monday. Red Lion, Appleby. Sailor and Landseer, self; "Ace," Stephen Goodall; Avenue, Stephen Shepherd. Small pack, 19½ couple; scent capital. Wind, N.E.; very cold.

Birdshill Gorse being cut down, Geo. Moore used to put a terrier through the earth, while the hounds drew the rough grass and nettles at the other end. Bolted a fox from the earth, came out of the top of the cover, turned to the left, and crossed the brook towards Measham Mill; ran up almost to the canal bridge as if for Willesley, turned to the left along the side of the brook to Stretton, which they crossed nearly opposite the house. Checked for a moment, but hit it off before anyone got to them, crossed the road to Ashby, ran very hard across the road from No-Man's Heath to Seckington. Ransom and Darling made a capital turn —Fencer, Matchless, Ringlet, President, Barmaid, and Nimble, all doing well. Checked for a moment at the road at the top of the new Thorpe cover—twenty-five minutes up to the first check. Ran on very pretty up to Thorpe, where they checked again at the road, hit it two fields on. Up jumped a hare; Plunder and some young ones at it; stopped them. Up got another; Prudence and Dewdrop after it. Royal hit the line off in the other direction through a sheepfold, and put us right again; through Thorpe Gorse (cut down), across a deep country up to the railroad near Wiggington (where my horse cast a shoe—I took the "Ace" from Goodall), crossed at a bridge, and began to run for him; came down to the Thame, near the hanging cover at Elford, ran along the bank for about two fields (Cheerful leading), crossed the river—horses could not get over—ran up nearly to Fisherwick, turned to the left over the meadows, where they ran him in view. He swam the river at Comberford Mill to return to the Atherstone side : the hounds viewed him in the water, and dashed in at him. They landed on an island, where they killed him. No one could get to them, but Novice brought the head on shore, and some others a pad or two. Time, one hour and fifteen minutes. A very good run, and a very pretty finish. Sailor carried me like a bird, and the "Ace" the last part. Edmund Peel went very well on a black horse, also Powell on a grey ; Hervey, Wilson, Lawrenson, &c. Powell got his horse in the Thame, and old Green nearly got drowned in fording it. Bass got a bad fall, and broke a rib. Hon. J. Macdonald, Henry Forester, Stanhope, &c., were out, and came from Lord Chesterfield's, Bretby Park.

Frost set in very hard in the afternoon. Sir Geo. Chetwynd gave me a cigar, the last I ever smoked. Killed eighteen brace, and six to ground, up to date.

J. A. T.

THE CHARNDON RUN WITH THE BICESTER.

Letter from COLONEL ANSTRUTHER THOMSON to GEORGE MOORE, ESQ., of Appleby, December 23rd, 1856.

I HAVE had such a run last Tuesday (Dec. 23rd) as I never saw before, so have taken a large sheet of paper to tell you all about it, and have, moreover, made a map

for your benefit, as you know the country. Met at
Charndon Common. Sharpish air, but fine, still
morning. Twenty couple white hounds; my pack.
Found two or three foxes in Charndon Wood, and I
intended as soon as we had made a row in the wood, to
cut away to the end where a fox generally breaks; however, before I got there, two were holloaed away. In
going up the ride I crossed two lines of foxes, and some
hounds broke away on each, so I arrived with only four
couple; however, they came dropping on, and as soon as
I got twelve couple, I went away with them. We had
just got over the Edgcot Road and down the hill, where
our fox had turned to the right, when something headed
him, and he turned back in front of the hounds, in the
same field with them, and away they went over those
fine grass fields. Somehow another fox appeared, and
the two ran close together up to the Grandon and
Marsh Gibbon Road. I had a bad start, being the
wrong side of a big fence, and only caught them there.
The fox had run up the road towards me, and gone
through the gate, opposite to which I came into the road.
The twelve couple on the line were two fields to my left,
and five couples scoring to the cry in the next field to
me, when I whistled the five couple, nicked the scent
first, and then away they went in earnest, seventeen
couple, over Marsh Gibbon field, all grass, very deep,
double fences and brooks. We began by crossing the
brook twice, and a double, which thinned the field down
to seven or eight, George Drake being first, Bill Holland
and myself and Ned Drake next, Henry Lambton and
Ned Harrison a little behind us, and I never saw anyone else. At the Ham Green road the fox ran up the
road a little way, the leading four couple flashed on and
missed the turn, but the body hunted the line through.

I did not get them together till we got to the Luggarshall road. Here Ransom made a drive up the furrow of a ploughed field (only the second we had seen), and then stopped as if she was shot. The fox had been headed by a plough, and turned short to the left. Nosegay, Governess, and one other, hunted the line, and I nicked in with the body in the field before them, and away they scored again. They ran up the Luggarshall and Piddington road for the length of two fields; the fox was headed and turned down to the right, Gallant making a good hit; the fox then shifted one furrow, Dreadnought, another young one, hitting that off. Twice the fox tried to make his point at Piddington village, but both times was headed by hedge cutters; but he tried it a field further on, and then turned up again, and set his head for Muxwell Hill. In the turn the body ran over it, but Nosegay carried it on, and never left the line. When we crossed the Piddington and Luggarshall road the second time, two or three horsemen joined, but I had no time to see who they were, two Drakes, Holland, and I having the best of it. When about half way up the hill the hounds paused among some cattle, but Blossom, Governess, and two others hunted it through. When they got to the top, hounds turned short to the right, and I lost sight of them for two fields. The hill is very steep, and I got into a very deep stubble field, so I pulled into a trot to ease my horse, and I went through a farmyard, when I found myself again in the field with the hounds, and above them, they having gone down the hill, and Ned Drake and Holland having gone with them. George Drake had followed me through the farmyard, and then joined the other two; I kept above them. We then crossed the Brill and Bicester road, which only has two

or three practicable places. I got one above the hounds,
and the others had to go to the bottom of the hill. I
was still one field above the hounds, when they turned
sharp to the left, and came up the hill to me, and I was
able to stand still for a few minutes, much to the
advantage of my horse. Here Tom Lowndes came to
me, but we had not much time to spare. They streamed
down the hill as if for Boarstoll Wood, but when they
got to the road, turned away from it along the road for
two hundred yards, Blossom and Governess hunting it
beautifully. On again over a little brook and up to
Arncot Little Wood—here the fox ran through a sheepfold, and was only one field before us; down the rack-
way through the cut part of the wood, then down the
outside on to Arncot Great Wood, where he went into
the ride through the gate—one hour and seven minutes
without a check to this point. Up the ride nearly to
the top, two Harrisons, Lambton, two Drakes, Lowndes,
Holland, and myself being then with them, and Mr.
Brown, of Piddington, joined us as we crossed his farm;
then through the top part, and away over the hill, never
having checked or divided, Governess leading them
down the hill to the Arncot river, where they rather ran
away from us. When we got to the Ambrosden road
I thought he was going for the ruins, and went round
by the road; however, on he went parallel to the Merton
road, Brown and I on the road looking out for him to
cross, and the others riding the line. At Ashley Bridge
farm he turned short to the left from the road and
towards the farm, probably being headed, and as we
turned into the field I expect he crossed the road—he
was then two fields before us. Hunted it on through a
ploughed field, and he then crossed the road opposite

the Merton earths, but passed them on to the village, crossed the road again, and ran down to the river side. Here we had our first check. One hour and thirty minutes to this point. Soon hit it off, and hunted him back towards the farmhouse. Now comes the worst part of the story: Morris, my second whip, here came in sight on my left; about six couple of hounds had the line on the left side of a thick double hedge, the rest of the hounds being on the wrong side. Just then Powell came up, meeting us with two couple of the hounds which had been left behind. He saw something move in the hedge, pulled his cap off, and capped the hounds on his side to a hare. "Be quiet," I shouted. In the meantime, Morris has stopped the others off the line, and got their heads up. There was a curdog barking in the farmyard, and three young hounds ran through the gate towards it from the other side, in front of those that had had the line. They had their heads up, and started to join them, thinking there was a view. I got them all quiet as soon as I could, and drew every hedge row round about for an hour, but could make no more of it. I got a line again over the road and up to the drain, and then away from it as if he had been headed, as there were two men working on the mouth of it almost, and I think since that he may perhaps have got in after all; at any rate, it was the best run I ever saw, and if we had caught him, would have been perfection. I was riding Maximus, Jack Darby's horse; he never made a mistake, but galloped the whole time with his head loose. He never was blown, and very little tired. Both he and I have a thorn in our knee, but that is all the grief we experienced. Come here, and we will try and do it again.

Col. Thomson rode Maximus and Peter; Tom Powell, Mayboy; Morris, Wolfdog. Twenty couple of white hounds.

N.B.—The Bicester packs were divided into white and black at that time.

THE WATERLOO RUN WITH THE PYTCHLEY,

FEBRUARY 2ND, 1866.

WRITTEN BY COLONEL ANSTRUTHER THOMSON.

THE accounts of the Waterloo Run have been so many and so various, that I send you what I believe to be the leading facts in the day's sport. The hounds ran their first fox in Loatland Wood, and in and out of cover for one hour and five minutes, and ran him to ground to Arthingworth. They found again in Waterloo Gorse at a quarter to two. The time from Waterloo to the earths at Keythorpe was one hour fifty minutes. The total time was three hours forty-five minutes, but we had a long check, twenty or twenty-five minutes at the windmill at Medbourne, and hunted on slowly afterwards. I take the distance to be from Waterloo to Kelmarsh, three miles; from Kelmarsh to Keythorpe, eighteen, as we ran it, being twenty-one miles in one hour and fifty minutes. There were only four ploughed fields in that distance. The hounds were only off the line once, between Kelmarsh and Keythorpe, when I lifted them one field to a holloa at Little Oxendon. As to changing foxes, I don't think we changed at Shipley Spinney. We might have changed when I lifted the hounds at Little Oxendon, but I don't think we did, as it was in the direction our fox was travelling. I think we changed at Keythorpe Wood, as another fox was viewed there besides the fox which we followed to Medbourne. We may have changed anywhere in a hedgerow, but I saw no perceptible change of scent, or anthing to cause me to think so. Some of your correspondents have asked where I managed to get five horses during the run. They will see in "Baily" that I was indebted to the kindness and sportsmanlike feeling of my friends, Mr. Hay and Mr. Walter de Whiton, and I beg all of them to accept my most grateful thanks. Both Colonel Frazer and Mr. Whyte, on getting fresh horses, also most generously offered them to me.

Friday, Feb. 2nd.—Met at Arthingworth. I rode Valeria and Rainbow; Dick Roake, Usurper; Tom Firr, Fresco; Charlie, my son, Amulet. I was staying at Sir Charles Isham's, at Lamport, and hounds called for me as they passed. A very wet morning, but cleared at eleven o'clock; very mild and still; not a very good scent in cover; wind, S.W. Found in Waterloo at five minutes past two by my watch (twenty minutes fast). The fox lay so still, I drew all round the cover, and back to the top before he moved. He lay among a heap of dead sticks—Graceful found him. Morris* holloaed him away towards the tunnel. I was at the other end of the cover, and before I got to the hounds they had checked near the road. I took them along the road nearly to the white gate, where they got the line towards Arthingworth. They were ridden off the line in the first field, but swung round through the fence on to it again, over the brook and spinney at Arthingworth, and crossed the rail. The field was full of sheep, and the shepherd told me the

---

* Richd. Morris, my second horseman, many years with Warwickshire and me, a capital man with hounds.

fox had gone into Langboro'. I carried them on, and just as I got to the gate he was holloaed away on the other side. I cut down the middle ride, and got on the line, crossed the Harboro' road, and ran fast on to Shipley Spinney. Hounds just crossed the end of the Spinney, and went right up the hill towards Clipston, and then it began in earnest. Dick went round the Tallyho end of the Spinney (Covert at west end of Shipley Spinney), and viewed another fox, and blew his horn, which distracted some of the field, and put them out of it. Two fields further on there was a stiff stile and footboard, which lots of fellows tumbled over. I had a shy at the bullfinch up hill, high and strong, and it turned Valeria over. I lost a spur, which I put in my pocket, picked up the pieces, and set sail, but I lost half a field, which I could not regain. Two fields on another stile, and lots of grief. Robertson No. 2 and another down, blocked the way. The field then divided into two lots, the right hand lot well with the hounds—Custance, Tom, Charlie Whyte, Frazer, Topham, and perhaps twenty more. The left hand lot, myself, Mills, De la Cour, Boyd, &c., about a field and a half behind the hounds. Hounds ran on without a pause past the spinney between Oxendon and Clipston, leaving Oxendon village to the right, into the Farndon and Oxendon road. I came into the road opposite Mr. Kirkman's house. They checked here, and I lifted them on to a holloa one field off, having to jump a nasty double, with a rail to me to get at it. Governess first spoke to the line, and off we went again, crossed the bottom from Farndon, which Vivian jumped first and foll; I scrambled in and out. Nethercote Whyte, Frazer, and Topham were first at the next fence. Hounds then began to go down the hill towards Lub-

benham, one field to the right of the Farndon and
Harboro' road. I got into the road, and here Dick and
Charlie (my boy) joined us. Hounds crossed the road
into the big field, and the Welland at the Harborough
corner. Charlie had a shy at the rails and tumbled over
them. I went further up the field for a broken rail.
Dick and I both lay to the left for Lubbenham cover,
thinking that was his point, but he crossed the river
and rail at the Harboro' end. We lifted the railway
gate off its hinges, and crossed near the cover—Topham,
Mills, Mayon, Charlie, &c. We caught the hounds at
the Harboro' and Lubbenham road. They then turned
their heads towards Bowden Inn, and began to run
hard. Grief began to be visible at the next fence, a
nasty place up hill. Birch Reynardson had his horse
in the ditch, and was exclaiming, "Oh, dear! oh, dear!"
Two fields further on my mare began to trot (she had
a good dressing with the first fox, having run an hour
up and down the rides in Loatland Wood). I heard
Dick whistle behind me, and say, "Take my horse, sir,
he has ten minutes left." I changed with him, and told
him to get "Rainbow" from Morris as soon as he could.
"Usurper," his horse, was fresh enough, for he rushed at
the first fence—a drop—over-jumped himself, and gave
me a regular burster, and knocked five minutes of the
ten out of himself. No harm done; scrambled on and
caught the hounds at the railway bridge at Bowden Inn.
The fox had run the road. Relish hit the line through
the hedge on the right, and Tom held the rest up to her.
The field had cut off the tail hounds, and got Flasher
and Graceful in the middle of them, and were playing
at football with them, for which I blessed them. They
ran round the back of Bowden Inn, paused for a
minute at a plough, and crossed the rail at the first

crossing right of the Langton road. Flasher first over the rail, and then over the brook, and on as if for Langton Caudle. Frank Langham went at the brook, and his horse jumped in. Tom Firr, seeing the bottom was good, jumped in and out. Custance jumped it well, just as Tom got out. Mills and I jumped it more to the right, in a watering place, and got over well, only two others, Langham and Tom, over before us. It caused lots of grief, and many took to the road at Bowden Inn. Whyte and Frazer's horses stand there, and they both got fresh horses. The fox was headed on the top of the next hill, and turned along the valley. Here Charlie Whyte came up on a fresh grey horse, and kindly offered to let me have it. We now began to be a mutual assistance society, and help each other, and pulled down rails and made gaps. Crossed the road between Thorpe Langton and Great Bowden; hounds still carried on steadily. I just saw Langton Caudle, which we left on our left, and thought it would be the end of the journey, and that I could just hug up to it. Crossed the Thorpe Langton and Welham road, got through the brook at a ford, going up a hill. Here Usurper dropped into a trot, and Mr. Hay lent me his horse, a brown thoroughbred. The first gate I came to half closed and touched its side; it plunged and pitched me clean over its head. We here came to a ploughed field and a wheat field. The field remained on the grass on the top of the hill. I went with the hounds, and had to jump a ditch up hill out of the plough. The horse did not land hind legs, and was not strong enough to get up, so I jumped off. At the bottom of the hill, a "Pat" holloaed us on—"Just gone when I holloaed;" and off again just over the grass, turned to the left past a brick kiln, crossed the road between Staunton Wyville and Cranoe, and up hill to a spinney. Hay's horse could gallop well, so I got on to the other side, stood still for a minute, and saw hounds come out, Royston hunting it single-handed through the sheep; and then Monarch spoke on the other side of the hedge, the rest came bundling on, and away we went, "Cherry" Angel here in company. Crossed a lane near Glooston village, and carried on well through several fields full of sheep. "Hurrah for the Duke of Beaufort!" said I—Ferryman,* guiding the scent, leading to Glooston Wood. "I always told you so," says Clerk (Tailby had been in it the day before). Through the wood like bells, and away on the other side towards Skeffington. Allan Young holloaed them away. On coming out of the wood I had a shoe off, and Walter de Winton changed horses with me. There is a nasty deep bottom at the end of the field, where Custance got his horse fast; my horse, or rather de Winton's, refused it, and Edgill scrambled in. Just then I heard Dick whistle, and found him on the other side on Rainbow. I jumped off, got over the rails, and set sail all right again. Some men rabbiting had turned the fox half a field to the left, and they ran clear away from us again. John Chaplin and another were before me, but kept too far to the left. I got along the road to Godeby with Colonel Mayon, and caught them at the corner of the road, and then went on with them alone to Keythorpe Wood. Here they checked a moment in the wood, or at least did not speak. I got on to the middle ride, and saw Singer, Streamer, and Ferryman cross, but not on the line; however, they hit it off again, and went away towards Ramshead. I got the rest after them, and had eleven couple on—Fanny the last hound out. Dick and Tom both there. Three

---

* Ferryman, by Duke of Beaufort's Finder.

fields further on the fox tried the earth, where Tailby had run to ground on the previous Tuesday, and dug out. I looked at my watch : one hour and fifty minutes, and, I think, about eighteen miles, and hounds had only once been off the line, when I lifted them at Little Oxendon. Here there was something like two lines, the body of the hounds going down the field towards Ramshead ; a few others had a scent on the right-hand side of the hedge. Coventry joined us somewhere here, with a pair of trousers on. I heard Tom, a field behind me, holloa, " Yonder he goes ! " and, at the same time, Colonel Frazer told me one-and-a-half couple of hounds were two fields on to the right. I thought the fox had gone through Hallaton Thorns—there is a deep bottom and very steep hill here. I lifted the hounds (hoping to catch the leading ones there) to the far side of Hallaton Thorns. When I got half way up the hill, two gentlemen on foot, who were rabbiting, showed me where the leading hounds were ; they had not come into Hallaton, but were pointing for Fallow Closes, along outside the fence, in at the gate, and then away along the bottom. I only got thirteen couple away from here, Merryman, Streamer, Relish, Ransom, Dragon, Singer, generally leading, and all working well. Frantic, though she had not been out for weeks, was there. We passed Mr. Studd's house, and they ran away from us again down to Slawston Covert—they just came out of the cover as we got there. The field was full of sheep, and they got the line at the cross-roads. While we were on the road some men on the hill viewed the fox going along the hollow behind us, only one field off. We cut along the road, and got on the line directly, run hard down the meadows to the Welland, near the angle of the river at Welham ; turned to the

left along the bank of the river, as far as the road which
goes to Medbourne station, there turned to the left up
to the windmill, and got on to ploughed land. Here
Captain Clerk turned up. The fox had been coursed
by a sheep dog, and repeatedly turned. This caused a
long check (perhaps twenty minutes). A man told me
he had gone slantways across a large wheat field (which
was wrong), and after holding the hounds all round it,
I got the line straight on again in the direction we had
formerly been going, but with a failing scent. The
hounds crossed the line without acknowledging it : Relish
stopped back alone, and made a drive down the furrow
without speaking to it. I put the rest on to her, and
in the next field they began to hunt it again, but they
could not go the same pace as before. They crossed the
road between Medbourne and Hallaton, and ran up the
side of the brook to the road which goes to Blaiston,
Graceful being the last hound to hit off the line; she
had also been the first one to speak to it in the morning.
It was then almost dark, and I was afraid we might
lose the hounds, so I stopped them at 5.30, having run
three hours and forty-five minutes. There was a halloa
about two fields on at the time. Mr. Piercy, the clergyman at Slawston, had come out on foot when he heard
the hounds. He took us to his house and refreshed us,
gave the horses gruel, and treated us hospitably, and
most kindly offered me a hack if I wished to leave my
horse, but he was not tired, and carried me home quite
cheerfully. He carried me more than two hours,
and never made a mistake—a pretty good trial for
a five-year-old. I had gone on for an hour and
forty-five minutes without a whipper-in, or having
the hounds turned to me once. Captain Clerk, who
was the only man who went through on one horse,

helped me through Market Harborough; all the rest of the way we jogged side by side, and the hounds trotted along with their sterns up. It was a fine, mild, quiet night. I stopped every three or four miles, and called them; they all came round me, wagging their tails, and trotted on again. We got to the kennels, eighteen or nineteen miles, about ten o'clock.

At Lamport I met all the party starting for the Harborough ball. My wife returned, and waited while I went to Brixworth with the hounds, got a hack, and galloped back to Lamport. I met Dick with "Usurper," just as I was coming out of Brixworth. I sat down to dinner at ten minutes to eleven o'clock, got to the Harborough ball at 12.30, and remained two hours. I was very little tired, and was at Ashby St. Legers by twelve o'clock the next day.

After I changed horses with Dick at Glooston, he came on with Mr. Hay's horse to the top of Hallaton Thorns, but finding he could not go the pace to be any assistance, he came quietly on to Fallow Closes, picked up Tyrant (who was short of work, having a toenail off,) and Bluecap, and went to Mr. Hay's, at Great Bowden. He there got his own horse, who had eaten a feed of corn, went into Harborough to get a shoe put on, and jogged on home. Charlie went as far as Langton, overtook Morris at Bowden Inn, and went home with him. Tom's horse, "Fresco," carried him capitally up to Keythorpe, and there he stopped trying to get up to me, when he viewed the fox. He came on as far as Slawston, and then went on to Bowden Inn, where his horse remained all night. John Pye, my groom, came on the carriage to Harborough when we went to the ball, and brought him home next morning. Of the hounds left out, Bowman, Fanny, Governess, and Glory, came home next day; Monarch came in on Monday.

I never could see the fox or get any advantage on him, and I don't think I lost a chance. At Keythorpe we may have changed, for Tom saw a fox besides that which the hounds were on. Tailby had been in Glooston Wood the day before. There was no check or perceptible change of scent.

This was the best run I ever saw, and over the finest country and longest distances, straight. There was one ploughed field between Waterloo and Kelmarsh; the second was next the railway behind Bowden Inn. There was a wheat field and a ploughed field together near Cranoe, and I don't think the hounds were ever off grass, with these exceptions, up to the earth at Keythorpe—one hour and fifty minutes.

The hounds worked well, chasing and carrying a good head up to Bowden Inn, hunting steadily through sheep and all difficulties; they were very fit to go, and not an ounce too much flesh. They did a wonderful day's work, having run their first fox an hour and five minutes before they began with this.

Yours truly,
J. A. T.

HOUNDS OUT.

Pytchley Hounds.		Young Hounds.
Regent	Singer	Dragon
Monarch	Streamer	Flasher
Falstaff	Statesman	Folly
Pilgrim	Tasty	Frantic
Governess	Tyrant	Glory
Gambler	Dashwood	Gossamer
Plunder	Driver	Gaiety
Royston	Druid	

Ferryman—Beaufort		Bluecap Graceful }	Meynell
Merryman Ransom }	Fitzwilliam	Romeo Promise }	Warwickshire
Relish Singer }	Bramham	Bowman—Lothian	
Fanny Lancer }	Lord Henry Bentinck		

THE LUNDIN RUN WITH THE FIFE HOUNDS,
NOVEMBER 30TH, 1877.

The meet was at Lundin Station, and here were
assembled, at eleven o'clock, the devotees of the chase.
* * * But now to the covert close at hand, and the
hounds are scarcely in it before you can tell that something is up. No fox is viewed away, but it is clear they
can smell one. After a flash in the wrong direction by
some of the youngsters, owing partly to excitement and
partly to a hare, they quietly got together again, and
with two or three cheery notes from the master's horn,
are out of the wood, and streaming away with a rattling
scent towards Durie—gently over that wall, with the
drop that lands you clear of the covert. If you don't
hit it and fall, you have taken your station in society
for the next two miles, and it will be your own fault if
you lose it. There is no doubt about it : this is not one
of your "hold hard, gentlemen," days ; you may ride
where you like, and the heart of the master rejoiceth.
* * * The pack stopped mute at an open drain.
Many are the devices suggested for the ejection of poor
Reynard : but cold water proves at once the most harm-
less and the most effectual, for in a few minutes, as if

refreshed by his bath, away he goes, and eighteen couple of hounds are in full chorus behind him. Torloisk is his point, which he reaches in safety, but not much to spare, and here it must be a moot point whether we changed foxes or not—at all events, the hounds were never for an instant off the line, it may be of a fresh, but I am inclined to think of our hunted fox, and taking it right through the covert, race away through Milldean Strips to Rameldrie. Here there was a slight check, but scarcely more than sufficient to allow of their carrying the scent through this thick covert of gorse and broom. When gallantly breasting the hill, it seemed at first as if they were making for Downfield or the Lime-works, but, suddenly turning north, he made again for the low country, and, sinking the hill, ran down straight to Ramornie. The turn was so short, that only three horsemen, viz., the Master, Col. Babington, and Mr. William Blackwood—who happened to get the direction the hounds had taken from the signals of a ploughman—were left in pursuit, and, let it be added, never fairly caught them. Through Melville woods and Park, close by the house and through the garden, this straight-necked fox held on till past Lindores, Dunbog, and Glenduckie. This wonderful chase came to an end on the banks of the Tay. Whether the hounds killed their quarry or not will never be known, but it will be remembered for many a long day, that Colonel Anstruther Thomson found a fox on the banks of the Forth and ran him to the banks of the Tay; and though he did not return home laden with the spoils of his enemy, still I venture to think that the chase of November 30th, 1877, will deservedly hold a very high place among his other great achievements.

HISTORY OF THE FIFE FOXHOUNDS.

HUNTING SONG OF MR. MEYNELL'S TIME, *

ABOUT 1790.

This morning at work, sowing out of my hopper,
Troth! who should come by but Dick, the earth-stopper.
Stop! Hark ye! says he, I think there be hounds:
Ods Bobs! they are Meynell's; I hear his Gad zounds.
  (Repeat)   With my Ballina mona ora,
        Squire Meynell's the hunter for me.

If we head him he'll d— us. We view! Tally ho!
Whilst the hounds ring the scent from the valley below,
All carrying a head, Sir, like pigeons in flight,
And beating the red coats almost out of sight.
        The hounds of Squire Meynell for me.

From the Coplow they came, and to Enderby go;
Then let us observe who rides over them now;
Then cease, my dear Squire, oh! cease your alarm,
For by Gosh! there's no rider can do them much harm.
        Squire Meynell's the hunter for me.

The first in the burst, see! yonder comes Maynard,
Taking all in his stroke, yet's obliged to strain hard.
And next him, on Marquis, there's dashing Charles
    Windham,
At a mortal great stride, leaving numbers behind him.
        The lads of Quorendon for me.

---

*Mr. Delmé Radcliffe mentions this as "a very old song," and says it was called "A Burst from Breedon Clouds," but in the printed copy kindly lent me by Mr. Cradock, of Quorn, it is only entitled "Hunting Song."

Then, funking his soul out, see Featherstonehaugh,
Who thin as a thread is, and light as a straw;
And screwing behind him, there's Fitzherbert's Dick,
His horse half done up, looking sharp for a nick.
    The lads of Quorendon for me.

Next Dick Knight and Smith Assheton we spy in the van,
Riding hard as two furies at catch that catch can.
"Now Egmont,"(1) says Assheton; "Now Contract,"(2)
    says Dick,
"By Gosh! these d——d Quornites shall now see the trick."
    No Northamptonshire hunters for me.

Now smack at a yawner rides Winchilsea's Peer,(3)
So sure to be thrown on Pyramid's ear;
And at the same place rides Smith, of Loraine;
He's off—no—he's on—he hangs by the mane.
    The lads of Quorendon for me.

Where Villiers and Forester, Cholm'ley and all,
Get shopp'd by Loraine, and in they all fall;
And sweety Morant, that red-headed ——
With Peyton and Foley, are left in a ditch.
    The lads of Quorendon for me.

Now plump on the saddle see Boothby, (4) the great;
Why, he's nervous this morning, and rides for a gate;
And, not less plump, sits friend Bobby Spencer, (5)
On thumping old Milo, and bilking the fence, Sir.
    The lads of Quorendon for me.

1. A famous hunter of Assheton Smith's.
2. A celebrated hunter, rode by Dick Knight, Lord Spencer's huntsman.
3. George, 8th Earl of Winchilsea, and 4th Earl of Nottingham, K.G.,
Lord Lieut. County Rutland succeeded 1769; died 1826, unmarried.
4. "Prince" Boothby, (lived with Mr. Meynell at Langton Hall.)
5. Lord Robert Spencer.

Then ecce Prince Orlines,(6) who's a la distance,
Without his d—d head, which is freedom in France;
But alas! long before they reach Burrow Hill
Monsieur blows his 'orse to von total stan' still.
   No Frenchified hunters for me.

Now bobbing along, see jolly fat Blower,(7)
Flanks and shoulders all blood, going slower and slower.
" Sarvant, your Holiness, what both a head and a shoe?
Thank God, I'm not last, for I've beat Parly vous."
   The lads of Quorendon for me.

Then, half up the hill, stops heavy Jew Francore,
His horse taking root, and himself at an anchor;
And further beyond stops White Bread,(8) the brewer,
Who, last from the first, has made the Grand Tour.
   The lads of Quorendon for me.

Then smoke the old Quiz, beginning to flag,
Somerset, Gad Zooks! on his new staring nag:
Why look ye! observe! he a toe can scarce wag,
Yet of him to-morrow friend Charley will brag.
   The lads of Quorendon for me.

Next vaulting Tam Grah'm,(9) on horse taking whim,
Plunging and prancing like the George at an inn,
Comes spank thro' a hedge with a thundering crush,
And leaves half his brogues and a lug on a bush.
   The lads of Quorendon for me.

---

6. Prince of Orleans.   7. A woolcomber, of Leicester.
8. The late Samuel Whitbread.   9. The present Lord Lynedoch.

Next chimney chops Aston, using arms, spur, and whip,
To keep Moll Cook's legs from plunging each grip;
Makes he on to three rails, where sticks little Hugo,
Who, glad to give way, says, " Pray Sir, do you go."
So Smut breaks his neck, and young Master Hug
Slides over as snug as a bug in a rug.
Then Commodore Harvey, on horse he can't guide,
Bears to the same gap, at a seamanlike stride;
Steers o'er the dead lubber, and makes three fresh wounds,
And at the next place kills all the tail hounds.
      The lads of Quorendon for me.

Then next, with a star on, see Bassador Gordon,(10)
And over his shoulder a fine flaming cordon;
And racing against him, see stare-about Stair; (11)
Why old Nick himself never saw such a pair.
      The lads of Quorendon for me.

Then whence these goose-drivers, all in a row,
Leading their tits on the furlongs below?
'Tis Cranberry,(12) George,(13) and Saint Le Hedger (14)
    from Grantham,
Who always get dos'd with their quotums and quantum.
      The lads of Quorendon for me.

Then far in the rear we see Saville, forlorn,
All legs, laps and lappets, sobbing on Roan;
How they stick in the mud; whilst Bedford's great Duke,
With Brommell, is sticking in Sysonby brook.
      The lads of Quorendon for me.

10. Sir William Gordon, Ambassador to Vienna.
11. Ambassador to Poland (John, 5th Earl of Stair, born 1749; died 1821.
Succeeded to the title 1789, which shows the song to be written after that
date).
12. Sir Carnaby Haggerstone, commonly called Cranberry Tart.
(Succeeded 1777; died 1831.)
13. Lord George Cavendish (who with Mr. Boothby was at first the only
other subscriber to Mr. Meynell's hounds.)
14. Colonel St. Ledger.

Next a tickle-heel sportsman, called Heyrick the black,
We descry in the vale, half a league from the pack ;
And further beyond, see Heyrick the white,
A sportsman by system, who never rides straight.
    The lads of Quorendon for me.

Then, last in the cluster, see Worcester (15) and Muster ;
Now Worcester beats Muster, (16) now Muster sets
    Worcester ;
Now Muster seems burst, Sir, and Worcester gets first,
    Sir ;
Such fumblers as these be ought both to be curst, Sir.
    The lads of Quorendon for me.

But Bob Lee, where's he, and wood-fisted Cox ?
Why they'll tell you they stopp'd to hallo the run fox ;
But so broad as the Smite is, we guess they got flung there,
And are shopped in a barn, with friend Arthur at Plungar.
    The lads of Quorendon for me.

Now cheering all Nature, Squire Meynell we spy,
Making ev'ry heart thrill with his "Hark to the cry!"
Look how he caps them on, hear how he screams,
And makes the whole world glow in rapture's extremes.

        See now they seem to spread—
        Lord, what a noble head !
    Tally ho! Tally ho! the hounds in full cry !
        See how the scent they drive,
        No horse can with them live.
    Hark away! Hark away! they to Enderby go.

---

15. Henry Charles, Marquis of Worcester, afterwards 6th Duke of
Beaufort, born 1766 ; succeeded 1803.
16. John Musters, of Colwick, born 1754, died 1827 ; father of the
celebrated gentleman huntsman, John Musters, born 1777.

Next, thumbs up, heels down, see Conyer's Jack,
So rosy, so active, pushing right 'cross the pack;
Cracking and whooping, "'Ware poison! 'ware nox!"
Which drove Meynell stark mad, and lost us the fox.

Then, as we trudge home, we pass Master Swaddle,
Whipping Pastime before him, and carrying the saddle:
"Good people," says he, "do you think she will die
Now I've bled her myself, in her mouth and her thigh?"

"Now let's to this ale-house," says Dick, "for awhile,
And drink our old Maister in a cup of the mild;
And as we sit boozing it over the fire,
Drink long life, health, riches, and sport to the Squire."

By MR. LORAINE SMITH.

Mr. Delmé Radcliffe, in that fascinating work, called
"The Noble Science of Foxhunting," gives the following
particulars of Mr. Loraine Smith, the author of the
preceding poem :—

"Of Mr. Loraine Smith, as a sportsman, it is unnecessary to speak. We may gather his character, in some
part, from the verses of several songs. * * *
The horse he rode on the day of the Billesdon Coplow
run was purchased of Mr. Cave Brown. He was a
brilliant hunter, got by Mercury. He was sold to Mr.
Fox Lane's father, at Bramham. Mr. Loraine Smith
was a skilful master of his pencil; and beneath a
painting, descriptive of the chase, appears the following
faithful record of this run :—

"A view of Mr. Meynell's hounds, carrying a head
with their second fox, at the end of a chase from
Billesdon Coplow, Leicestershire: passed Tilton Woods,

Skeffington Earths, crossing the river Soar below
Whitstone, to Enderby Warren, making a distance of
twenty-eight miles, which was run in two hours and
fifteen minutes, on Monday, February 24th, 1800.

"I conclude this memoir with a laughable epitaph
upon the Enderby Squire, written some years previous
to his death, by a Mr. Monro, with a rejoinder by
another talented friend, Mr. Heyrick :—

"Here lies the tall Squire of Enderby Hall,
With his bridles, boots, fiddle, brush, colours and all.
Some liked his scraping, tho' none of the best;
And all liked the welcome he gave to his guest.
His taste was, in horses and hounds, orthodox,
And no man can say he e'er headed the fox.
In the dog days, or frost, when the kennel was mute,
Each turn with the turn of his humour to suit;
As the weather still changed, still his plans he would
    change,
Now be-rhyming some Stella, now curing the mange.
Now the State he'd reform, now mend an old door,
Now scrawl a lampoon, now a caricature.
Ever last down at dinner, and first at a snore:
Sure enough he had faults, but his faults are now o'er.
Lack aday! that our Enderby Squire should be lost!
Can't you guess what he died of? a bitter hard frost."

THE SQUIRE'S RESURRECTION, BY HEYRICK, ESQ.

"Oh! how could you bury our neighbour so soon?
Why, his boots were just black'd and his fiddle in tune;
As a staunch, steady sportsman, and quite orthodox,
He'd been taking a glass to the hounds and the fox:
In his moments of mirth, he would sometimes drink deep;
When you thought he was dead, he was only asleep!"

Mr. Loraine Smith died the 23rd of August, 1835,
in the 85th year of his age.

A LEGEND OF THE QUORN COUNTRIE.

When, careful of his goods or spouse,
A strong man armed doth keep his house,
It may be termed for him a bore
To find a stronger at his door,
Who binds the strong man at his ease,
Pockets his cash and all he sees;
And tho' he does not take his life
Is far from civil to his wife.
The ex-strong man looks on the while
Without the least desire to smile;
At least, I take it such would be
The case, did such things chance with me.

There lived—I do not deal with dates—
A champion * of the heavy weights,
Who over Leicestershire had done
Great things in spite of sixteen stone;
For many years had been admired
For going when the rest were tired;
Who fear'd no timber, liked a brook,
Could calmly at a bullfinch look,
And thought himself in all his glory
Just at the period of my story.

But often when we feel most sure
We're apt to be the least secure,
And Gilmour, happy and content,
With long established precedent,
By all men honoured and respected,
Was rivall'd when he least expected.

---

* Mr. Little Gilmour.

'Twas in November's dreary sky
Strange meteors were seen to fly,
And rumour spread through all the land
That some convulsion was at hand;
And presently the fact was known
That one who weighed good seventeen stone,
Light of hand and firm of seat,
Arrived at Quorn, was bad to beat.

Well, all men deemed the fact absurd,
And Gilmour laughed at what he heard;
And not until he saw the man
The sinking in his boots began.

When first he shewed, beside the gorse,
Colossal seem'd his coal-black horse;
His frowning brow and deep-set eye
His heart's resolve did not belie.
Not oft he smiled, but if a trace
Of mirth did flit across his face
No joy, I ween, it might impart,
But chill'd the shuddering gazer's heart;
And Gilmour, at that harrowing look,
Down to his very small clothes shook,
When towards him with the lightning's speed
The stranger spurred his fiery steed.

" My name," he said, " is Peter Miles,†
And there is none like me
From Land's End to Northumberland
And all the North Countrie.

---

† Colonel Charles Miles.

" You Melton men, ye Leicester knaves,
Come ride with me, say I,
Five minutes over Skeffington,
And then lie down and die.

" I've heard of you, Sir Gilliemore,
I know you 're all my eye ;
I'll cut you down, and hang you up,
Aye, hang you up to dry !

" You funking wretch, I know you,
How you shudder at a rail !
How you shun the bristly bullfinch,
And at a brook turn tail.

" So here I seize your trophies
With every mark of scorn,
And hang up your reputation
In the dining room at Quorn."

He ceased—I fear my voice must fail
To tell the sequel of my tale :
But he who was not wont to brook
A hasty word or angry look,
Now, with a meek submissive face,
Yielded the trophies of the chase ;
Without a blow resigned his sway,
And Miles, triumphant, leads the way.
Thenceforth from gates and brooks he shrunk,
Thenceforth by all was called a "funk."
Such is the fate of human glory,
Such the sad sequel to my story.

I cannot tell the year of grace
In which these things were taking place ;
But this I know, a portly Squire
Now bruises over Leicestershire,
Whom Sutton ‡ loveth to commend
His " Guide, Philosopher and Friend,"
And none with him dispute the right
To lead the field from morn to night.
But tho' among the thrusting train
You seek for Gilmour's face in vain,
Wait till the second horsemen pass,
You see a form—tis his, alas !
A heavy man who funks the stiles,
And shudders at the name of " Miles."

MORAL.

Such is the lot of mortal man !
Where Gilmour ended, Miles began ;
And Miles in turn must yield his sway,
For " every dog must have his day."

W. DAVENPORT BROMLEY.

HUNTING SONG OF SIR HARRY GOODRICKE'S TIME.

The lark forgets her summer song,
  The rose forgets its bloom,
And murky clouds are borne along
  To aid the wintry gloom.

---

‡ Sir Richard Sutton hunted the Quorn country from 1847
till his death in 1855.

The woods, where nature hung her lute
  To teach sweet birds her tone,
Are hush'd; the sylvan groves are mute;
  The hills are pensive grown;

The dancing ripples of the lake
  Are changed to sullen waves;
The solitary water-crake
  Its cheerless bosom laves.

But joy awakes the sluggish morn,
  The mists now melt away;
The huntsman blithely winds his horn,
  The willing hounds obey.

Sir Harry's (1) forward in the field,
  Greene,(2) Gardner,(3) sportsmen true!
And more to whom bright fame must yield
  The praises justly due.

Lord Wilton,(4) Stanley,(5) Errington,(6)
  Seem scarce to touch the rein,
As gallantly they rush along
  O'er hill and grassy plain.

---

1. Sir Harry Goodricke, died 1833.
2. Mr. Greene, of Rolleston, afterwards Master of the Quorn Hounds from 1841 to 1847.
3. Lord Gardner, died 1883.
4. Lord Wilton, died 1884.
5. Mr. Massey Stanley, Mr. Errington's brother.
6. Mr. Errington, afterwards Master of the Quorn Hounds from 1835 to 1838.

"There's Greene, as usual, far before,"
   Cries handsome Edward Thynne; (7)
Kinnaird,(8) and Rokeby,(9) and Gilmour—(10)
   By Jove, I must nick in!"

He said, then urged his gallant steed,
   No fence for him too high;
He look'd the true bold hunter bred—
   "Yoiks, yoiks, the fox shall die!"

" Maher (11) and Moore (12) still take their stand
   High in the list of fame,
And friendship wreathes the social band
   With Musgrave's (13) sporting name.

Melton! again that sportsman's town
   Boasts many a noble guest;
Statesmen and heroes of renown
   The exulting soil have pressed.

Long, long may we those names enrol,
   And Goodricke's (14) lend a grace,
For fame to waft from pole to pole
   The triumphs of the chase.

From the SPORTING MAGAZINE FOR 1841.

---

7. Lord Edward Thynne.
8. Lord Kinnaird.
9. Lord Rokeby.
10. Mr. Little Gilmour, living 1885.
11. Valentine Maher, died 1844.
12. Mr. Moore, son of the Archbishop of Canterbury.
13. Sir James Musgrave.
14. Sir Harry Goodricke, died 1833.

BILLESDON COPLOW.

MONDAY, FEBRUARY 24TH, 1800.

" Quæque ipse miserrima vidi, et quorum pars magna fui."

With the wind at north-east, forbiddingly keen,
The Coplow of Billesdon ne'er witness'd, I ween,
Two hundred such horses and men at a burst—
All determin'd to ride, each resolv'd to be first.
But to get a good start over eager and jealous,
Two-thirds at the least of these very fine fellows
So crowded and hustled, and jostled and cross'd,
That they rode the wrong way, and at starting were lost.
In spite of th' unpromising state of the weather
Away broke the fox and the hounds close together;
A burst up to Tilton, so brilliantly ran,
Was scarce ever seen in the mem'ry of man:
What hounds gained the scent, or which led the way,
Your bard, to their names quite a stranger, can't say,
Tho' their names, had he known, he is free to confess
His horse could not shew him at such a death pace.
Villiers, Cholmondeley, and Forrester made such sharp
  play,
Not omitting Germain, never seen till to-day;
Had you judged of these four by the trim of their pace
At Bib'ry you'd think they'd been riding a race.
But these hounds, with a scent, how they dash and they
  fling!
To o'er-ride them is quite the impossible thing.
Disdaining to hang in the Wood, thro' he raced,
And the open for Skeffington gallantly faced,
Where, headed and foiled, his first point he forsook,
And merrily led them a dance o'er the brook.

Passed Galby and Norton, Great Stretton and Small,
Right onward still sweeping to old Stretton Hall,
Where two minutes' check serv'd to shew, at one ken,
The extent of the havoc 'mongst horses and men:
Such sighing, such sobbing, such trotting, such walking,
Such reeling, such halting, of fences such baulking;
Such a smoke in the gaps, such comparing of notes,
Such quizzing each other's daub'd breeches and coats.
Here a man walked afoot who his horse had half killed,
There you met with a steed who his rider had spill'd;
In short, such dilemmas, such scrapes, such distress
One fox ne'er occasion'd, the knowing confess.
But, alas, the dilemmas had hardly begun!
On for Wigston and Ayleston he resolute ran,
Where a few of the stoutest now slacken'd and panted,
And many were seen irretrievably planted.
The high road to Leicester the scoundrel then cross'd,
As Tell Tale (1) and Beaufremont (2) found to their cost;
And Villiers esteem'd it a serious bore
That no longer could Shuttlecock (3) fly as before.
Even Joe Miller's (4) spirit of fun was so broke
That he ceased to consider the run as a joke.
Then, streaming away, o'er the river he splashed,
Germain, close at hand, off the bank Melon (5) dash'd:
Why the Dun prov'd so stout in a scamper so wild—
Till now he had only been rode by a Child. (6)
After him plung'd Joe Miller, with Musters so slim,
Who twice sank and nearly paid dear for his whim,
Not reflecting that all water melons must swim.

---

1. Tell Tale.—Mr. Forrester's horse.
2. Mr. Maddock's horse.
3. Lord Villiers' horse.
4. Mr. Musters' horse.
5. Mr. Germain's horse.
6. Formerly the property of Mr. Child, to whom this Hunt is perhaps indebted for the present spirited style of riding to hounds.

Well sous'd by their dip on they brush'd o'er the bottom,
With liquor on board enough to besot 'em.
But the villain, no longer at all at a loss,
Stretch'd away like a devil for Enderby Gorse,
Where, meeting with many a brother and cousin,
Who knew how to dance a good hay in the furzen,
Jack Raven (7) at length, coming up on a hack
Which a farmer had lent him, whipp'd off the game
    pack.
Running sulky, old Loadstone (8) the stream would not
    swim,
No longer sport proving a magnet to him.
Of mistakes and mishaps, and what each man befell,
Would the Muse could with justice poetical tell!
Bob Grosvenor on Plush, (9) tho' determin'd to ride,
Lost at first a good start, and was soon set aside:
Tho' he charg'd hill and dale, not to lose this rare chase,
On Velvet, Plush could not get footing, alas!
To Tilton sail'd bravely Sir Wheeler O'Cuff,
Where, neglecting thro' hurry to keep a good Luff,
To leeward he drifts—how provoking a case!
And was forc'd, tho' reluctant, to give up the chase.
As making his way to the pack's not his forte,
Sir Lawley, (10) as usual, lost half of the sport:
But then the professed philosophical creed,
That "All's for the best" of Master Candide,
If not comfort, Sir R. reconcile may at least,
For on this supposition his sport is the best.
Orby Hunter, who seem'd to be hunting his fate,
Got falls to the tune of no fewer than eight.

---

7. Jack Raven, the huntsman.
8. The huntsman's horse.
9. Mr. Robert Grosvenor's horse.
10. Sir Robert Lawley, not unusually, in the brief language of Melton, called Sir Lawley.

Basan's King (11) upon Glimpse, (12) sadly out of
    condition,
Pull'd up to avoid of being tir'd the suspicion.
He did right, for Og very soon found
His worst had he done, he'd have scarce glimps'd a
    hound.
Charles Meynell, who lay very well with the hounds,
Till at Stretton he nearly arrived at the bounds,
Now discover'd that Waggoner (13) rather would creep
Than exert his great prowess in taking a leap;
But when crossing the turnpike he read, "Put on here,"
'Twas enough to make anyone bluster and swear.
The Waggoner, feeling familiar the road,
Was resolv'd not to quit it, so stock still he stood.
Yet prithee, dear Charles, why rash vows do you make,
Thy leave of old Billesdon (14) to finally take?
Since from Seg's Hill (15) for instance, or p'r'aps
    Melton Spinney,
If they go a good pace you are beat for a guinea.
'Tis money, they say, makes the mare to go kind—
The proverb has vouch'd for this time out of mind;
But tho' of this truth you admit the full force,
It may not hold so good of every horse.
If it did, Ellis Charles need not hustle and hug
By name, not by nature, his favourite Slug. (16)
Yet, Slug as he is, the whole of this chase
Charles ne'er could have seen had he gone a snail's pace.

---

11. Mr. Oglander, who, according to the same dialect, goes by the more
familiar appellation of Og.
12. Mr. Oglander's horse.
13. Mr. Charles Meynell's horse.
14. He had threatened never again to attempt following the hounds
from Billesdon, as no horse could carry his weight up to them in that part of
the country.
15. A very different part of the Hunt.
16. Mr. Charles Ellis's horse.

Old Gradus, (17) whose fretting and fuming at first,
Disqualified strangely for such a tight burst,
Ere to Tilton arriv'd ceas'd to pull and to crave,
And tho' freshish at Stretton he stepp'd a Pas grave,
Where, in turning him over a cramp kind of place,
He overturned George, whom he threw on his face;
And on foot to walk home it had sure been his fate,
But that soon he was caught, and tied up to a gate.
Near Wigston occurred a most singular joke:
Captain Miller avow'd that his leg he had broke,
And bemoan'd in most piteous expressions how hard,
By so cruel a fracture, to have his sport marr'd.
In quizzing his friends he felt little remorse,
To finesse the complete doing up of his horse.
Had he told a long story of losing a shoe,
Or of laming his horse, he very well knew
That the Leicestershire creed out this truism worms,
"Lost shoes and dead beat are synonymous terms." (18)
So a horse must here learn, whatever he does,
To die game, as at Tyburn, and "die in his shoes."
Bethel Cox and Tom Smith, Messieurs Bennet and
    Hawke,
Their nags all contriv'd to reduce to a walk.
Maynard's Lord, who detests competition and strife,
As well in the chase as in social life,
Than whom nobody harder has rode in his time,
But to Crane (19) now and then now thinks it no crime,
That he beat some crack riders most fairly may crow,

---

17. Mr. George Ellis's horse.
18. Indeed, so implicit is this article of the Meltonian belief, that many a horse, in addition to the misfortune of breaking a hoof from losing his shoe, has laboured likewise under the aforesaid unavoidable imputation, to his everlasting disgrace.
19. Crane.—The term derives its origin from the necessary extension of neck of such sportsmen as dare to incur the reproach by venturing to look before they leap.

For he liv'd to the end, though he scarcely knows how.
With Snaffle and Martingale kept in his rear,
His horse's mouth open half up to his ear,
Mr. Wardle, who threatened great things overnight, (20)
Beyond Stretton was left in most terrible plight :
Too lean to be pressed, yet egged on by compulsion,
No wonder his nag tumbled into convulsion.
Ah! had he but lost a fore-shoe, or fell lame,
'Twould only his sport have curtail'd, not his fame. (21)
Loraine, (22) than whom no one his game plays more
    safe,
Who the last, than the first, prefers seeing by half;
What with nicking (23) and keeping a constant look out,
Every turn of the scent surely turn'd to account.
The wonderful pluck of his horse surprised some,
But he knew they were making point blank for his
    home.
" Short home " to be brought we all should desire
Could we manage the trick like the Enderby Squire. (24)
Wild Shelley, (25) at starting, all ears and all eyes,
Who, to get a good start, all experiments tries ;
Yet contriv'd it so ill as to throw out poor Gipsy, (26)
Whom he rattled along as if he'd been tipsy ;

---

20. Who was said to have threatened that he would beat the whole field the next day.

21. For which express purpose, more than sport, some are silly enough to suppose he hunts ; and which, though he did actually succeed in one instance some seasons ago, he probably will never do again, having threatened it frequently since with as little success.

22. Mr. Loraine Smith.

23. A term of great reproach, according to the above dialect, to those who are so shabby as to cut across to the hounds, when it is esteemed so much more honourable to follow their very track ; by which spirited line of conduct they may be pretty certain of never seeing them at all.

24. Where Mr. Loraine Smith lives.

25. Sir John Shelley.—Wild with joy upon these occasions, must be here meant, as no one can be personally more serious and sedate ; indeed, if the worthy Baronet has a foible it is gravity.

26. Sir John Shelley's mare.

To catch them again, but tho' famous for speed,
She never could touch (27) them, much less get a lead.(28)
So dishearten'd, (29) disjointed, and beat, home he
swings,
Not much unlike a fidler hung upon strings.
An H. H., (30) who in Leicestershire never had been,
So of course such a tickler (31) ne'er could have seen,
Just to see them throw off, on a raw (32) horse was
mounted,
Who a hound had ne'er seen, or a fence had confronted.
But they found in such style, (33) and went off at such
score, (34)
That he could not resist the attempt to see more :
So with scrambling, (35) and dashing, (36) and one rattling
fall, (37)

27. Touch.—Meaning, according to the Melton dialect, overtake.

28. Get a lead.—By which it is to be understood securing the privilege of breaking your neck *first*, and when you fall, of being rode over by a hundred and ninety-nine of the best fellows upon earth, to a *dead* certainty.

29. Nor can that astonish anyone, when it is considered what an inestimable privilege he has lost.

30. It is not clear whether these initials are meant to apply to a Hampshire Hog or the Hampshire Hunt. If to the hog, it does not appear that he saved his bacon.

31. Tickler (Meltonian).—A run so severe that there is no laughing at it.

32. Raw.—A horse who knew nothing of the business he was going about, or wished to know.

33. Style means the best possible manner of doing anything : as for instance, when a man rides his horse full speed at double posts and rails, with a squire trap on the other side (which is a moderate ditch of about two yards wide, cut on purpose to break gentlemen's necks), he is then reckoned to have rode at it in style, especially if he is caught in the said squire trap.

34. Score means that kind of pace which perhaps neither you nor your horse ever went before, and if you have not more luck than falls to the share of every first experiment of the kind, 'tis ten to one but he falls before he can (what they call) get on his legs—in which case you may rest perfectly satisfied that he must roll over you two or three times at least before he can stop himself.

35. Scrambling means, when a horse does not leave above three of his legs behind him, and saves himself by pitching on his head.

36. Dashing means, when a man charges a fence (which no other word can express so fully), on the other side of which it is impossible to guess what mischief awaits him, but where his getting a fall is reduced as nearly as possible to a moral certainty.

37. Rattling fall, Q.E.D.

He saw all the fun up to Stretton's white hall.
There they anchor'd—in plight not a little distressing,
The horse being raw, he of course got a dressing.
That wonderful mare of Vanneck's, who till now
By no chance ever tir'd, (38) was taken in tow:
And, what's worse, she gave Van such a devilish jog
In the face with her head, plunging out of a bog,
That with eye black as ink, or as Edward's fam'd
    Prince,
Half blind has he been, and quite deaf ever since.
" But let not that mortify thee, Shacaback," (39)
She only was blown, (40) and came home a rare hack.
There Craven, too, stopp'd, whose misfortune, not fault,
His mare unaccountably vex'd with string-halt; (41)
And when she had ceas'd thus spasmodic to prance,
Her mouth 'gan to twitch with St. Vitus's dance. (41)
But how shall describ'd be the fate of Rose Price, (42)
Whose fav'rite white gelding convey'd him so nice
Thro' thick and thro' thin, that he vow'd and protested, (43)
No money should part them as long as life lasted?

38. Which, if other proof were wanting, ascertains beyond anything else the severity of this chase.

39. A familiar appellation, borrowed from Blue Beard, and bestowed by his friends at Melton on Mr. Vanneck, than whom nothing can more thoroughly prove the estimation in which his society is held there, since none but good fellows are ever esteemed, according to the Meltonian principles, worthy of a nickname.

40. Which was his own observation, the merit of which I would scorn to assume, but for the truth of which (at least the latter assertion) I can vouch, as I perfectly agree with him, that I never saw a more complete hack, though he is pleased to call her a hunter.

41—41. Two nervous affections, in every sense of the word very distressing, especially to a bystander who cannot command his risible muscles upon so melancholy an occasion.

42. A gentleman, of whom it has been commonly said, that he never returned from hunting but his horse was sure to be either lame or knocked up.

43. At the cover-side his horse had been particularly admired, and a considerable sum of money offered for him.

But the pace (44) that effected, which money could not,
For to part, and in death! was their no distant lot:
In a fatal blind ditch Carlo Khan's (45) prowess failed,
Where no lancet (46) nor laudanum (46) either availed.
More care (47) of a horse than he took could take no man,
He'd more straw than would serve any lying-in woman.
Still he died! Yet just how, as nobody knows,
It may truly be said, he died "under the Rose."
At the death of poor Khan, Melton (48) feels such
    remorse,
That they've christen'd that ditch, the Vale of White
    Horse!
Thus ended a chase, which for distance and speed
Its fellow we never have heard of or read;
Every species of ground every horse does not suit—
What's a good country hunter (49) may here prove a
    brute;

44. Which is a complete answer to that important question, so vauntingly asked by a favourite poet, when he exclaims, in language indeed somewhat bold,—"Pray, what can do that which money cannot?"

45. The name of poor Mr. Price's horse.

46—46. Two excellent restoratives where the patient is not too far gone; where he is (as in the present case), inimitable soporifics.

47. Indeed, it is only to be lamented, that Mr. P. had not taken rather more care of him a little earlier in the day, which probably would have obviated the necessity of this accouchement.

48. Which redounds highly to the credit and the sympathy of the Melton gentlemen, and completely refutes a very ill-natured but groundless supposition, that their sensibility will ever suffer them to make a joke of any such heavy loss a gentleman may happen to sustain, especially if the gentleman happens likewise to be heavy himself, which of course doubles the weight of the misfortune.

49. As every country gentleman may not comprehend the force of this expression, he ought to know that the Meltonians hold every horse who cannot "Go along a slapping pace"—"Stay at that pace"—"Skim ridge and furrow"—"Catch his horses"—"Top a flight of rails"—"Come well into the next field"—"Charge an oxfence"—"Go in and out clever"—"Face a brook"—"Swish at a rasper"—and in short, "Do all that kind of thing" which are all so plain and intelligible, that it is impossible to mistake their meaning,—that horse is held in the same contempt, in Leicestershire, as a coxcomb holds a country bumpkin. In vulgar countries (i.e., all others), where these accomplishments are not indispensable, he may be a hunter.

And unless for all sorts of strange fences prepared,
A horse and his rider are sure to be scared.
'Tis variety gives constant life to the chase,
But as Forrester (50) says, "Sir, what kills is the pace."(51)
In most other countries they boast of their breed,
For carrying, at times, such a beautiful head;
But these hounds to carry a Head cannot fail,
And constantly, too, for by George! there's no Tail. (52)
Talk of horses and hounds, and the system of kennel,
Give me Leicestershire nags and the hounds of Old
    Meynell.

By Mr. Lowth.

Memoir of the Mastership of the Fifth Duke of Buccleuch,

WALTER FRANCIS MONTAGU DOUGLAS SCOTT,

Born 1806; Died 1884.

His Grace, in 1824, when eighteen years of age (with the consent of his guardians), bought the hounds of Mr. Baird, of Newbyth (grandfather of the present Sir David), who continued to manage them until his Grace's majority in 1827, in which year he took up the country

---

50. A gentleman who practically explains all the above accomplishments, to the great edification of young horses and the no less astonishment of weak minds.

51. A favourite maxim of Mr. Forrester's, of the truth of which he seldom loses an opportunity of endeavouring to make his friends thoroughly sensible.

52. As heads and tails are here not to be understood in the common acceptation of the words, and as all ladies are not sportswomen enough to be aware that they have no reference to the human head or tail, they should know that, when you can "cover the hounds with a sheet" (which any Meltonian will explain to them more particularly), they are then said to carry a beautiful head. When (on the contrary) they follow the leader in a line, like a flight of wild fowl, they are then said to tail.

till then hunted by Mr. Baillie, of Mellerstain, which he hunted, unaided, until his death.

Frank Collinson hunted them for about a year after his Grace bought them, when, having a bad fall, Williamson, who had been first whip for about twelve years, and second for seven previously, became huntsman in the spring of 1825, and continued so until 1862. Tom Phillips succeeded him for one year, when he left, and I succeeded him in the spring of 1863; thus making his Grace a master of the same pack fifty-nine years. Collinson, who whipped-in to John King, succeeded him as huntsman, but did not continue long. He was pensioned by the Lothian Hunt, and lived for many years after, and chiefly rode young horses for his Grace with the hounds.

Old Will began life with Colonel Hamilton, of Pencaitland, in the stables, his father being groom. He entered to hounds under John King in 1815, afterwards marrying John King's daughter.

So primitive was kennel management in those days, that he has often told me how F. Collinson used to start off the night before hunting, with a knife and sack, going to where they knew a horse had died, skin the horse, score him (like scoring a piece of pork), and come that way home next day after hunting, and let the hounds have their bellyful of him, bringing the skin home in the sack in front of him on the horse. What would a whip of the present day say to you if you were to ask him to do this now? Williamson thought no shame in telling that he knew nothing at all about kennel management when he got the hounds (nor were any others about here then any fitter), and in order that he might learn something more about it, and his business, he *rode* to Eddlethorpe, near Malton, to engage a kennelman

from old Tom Carter, who hunted Sir Mark Sykes'
hounds then, and engaged John Fobert as feeder, and
had him at Dalkeith for several years, and all he ever
knew of kennel management he learned from him. He
was father of the trainer, John Fobert, who afterwards
trained for Lord Eglinton.

I am very glad you have asked me for those dates, as
I have had them so many times from the late Duke himself, who delighted to tell you anything connected with the
hounds and country; and from Williamson I think I
may have learned more about the country then and now
hunted by the Duke than you might now get from any
other quarter. As far as I could make out from him, the
hounds of that day were very much the same as his
Grace liked to have now—light, racing, rather leggy
hounds. Of late years they are shorter on the
leg, and a little more bone—what old Will and his
Grace to the last called *lumber*.

I hope these few notes may be of service to you. If
so, I will be very pleased.

(From Col. Anstruther Thomson.)

WILLIAM SHORE.

IN MEMORIAM.

GEORGE WHYTE-MELVILLE,

DIED 1878.

The engineer by his own petard slain,
The eagle pierced by shaft from his own wing,
Are plaintive fancies such as poets sing,
And touch the heart but coldly, thro' the brain.

But thou, dear George, in thine own sport thus ta'en,
In all the prime of manhood, and the swing
Of gallant gallop, struck stone dead! the thing
Appals and petrifies the mind with pain.
Bright, brave, and tender, poesy's pet child,
Romance and history's lore alike were thine;
Thy wit ne'er wounded, yet the contest won,
For at thy jests the gravest dullard smiled.
Last scion of an ancient Scottish line,
Whose "old folks" live to mourn their only son.

LORD ROSSLYN.

EXTRACT FROM "BAILY," 1871.

"WHY is it we so seldom hunt up to a fox on a cold
scent, and pick him up creditably at the end—so ordinary
an occurrence in countries where one would imagine it
more difficult of accomplishment? Captain Thomson
does, but no one else can. It is far from my business
to "crab" the hunting of the crack packs, but there
must be a solution to the problem somewhere. Un-
doubtedly the perfection of a run in these parts is five
and twenty minutes, with a scent over which hounds
need not falter throughout, and a kill in the open of
course adds brilliancy to it. This is the sort of thing
that men come down to Leicestershire to see—that they
go out every day in hopes of—that is not often to be met
with even there; but, when experienced, brings with it
a supreme delight that is not to be found anywhere else.
A long slow run in a flying country is often irksome in
the extreme, particularly when it degenerates into
hedgerow hunting; but it too often happens that, as

soon as hounds cease to go fast, losing the fox instead
of killing him becomes merely a matter of time. Mind,
I do not say as soon as hounds have to put their heads
down, which is the form in which detractors of the "cut
'em down" countries couch their attacks; for I believe
herein lies part at least of the explanation. My idea is,
that so long as grass retains a scent at all, hounds can
move quick over it, and improve it as they go along; in
other words, that when they can run at all they can run
fast, and that when there is such a failure of scent as
to cripple them, they would not be able to own it at all on
the plough. The Midlands are by no means uninterrupted
grass, so one has frequent opportunity of observing
that when hounds seem to be carrying a fair head over
the turf, a fallow or two stops them at once. Another
thing is, that foxes take a great deal more killing here
than they do elsewhere; they are of a stouter breed
(most districts having at sometime or other been stocked
with bold Highlanders), and from the distance apart,
and the small extent of the covers, they travel
more, and are always fit to go before hounds; so
if they once get ahead and able to take their own time,
they are by no means easily overhauled. The real way
to kill foxes in the Shires is to get away close at them,
and burst them at starting. The scent is then hot and
firm, the hounds are not over-ridden by the field, the
foxes have no time to twist or run cunning, and, be it
a good scenting day or a bad one, there is more chance
of accounting for them than by trusting to slow hunting.
But in order to do this, a huntsman must have his pack
under perfect command, and it is absolutely essential
that he should be effectively whipped up to. To this
talent of getting his hounds quickly to him does Gillard
owe his success, and through it has he so often been able

to provide sport in accordance with the taste of the present day.

"The best run the Belvoir had last season was on the 15th of February, when, starting from Coston Covert, they hunted steadily for between two and three hours (I forget the exact time), going well for the greater part, and after reaching and traversing the woods of Morkery, and completely "sewing up" all single horses, at last killed in Gunby Warren. The hounds appeared to be never once off the line; and the opinion that they had not changed on the road was strengthened by their fox being as stiff as a board when taken from the hounds—a thing one often hears of, but seldom sees. Let credit be given where credit is due. Their huntsman, Gillard, is undeniable. Starting originally from the Belvoir, he went to school under Mr. Musters, who taught him his work in Nottinghamshire, and then brought him to handle his lady-pack over the Quorn grass. Here for two seasons he did justice to his hounds, country, and Master, and has now mounted the top step of the ladder. He has a whip, too, who has learned to put hounds to him as quick as lightning. Without a good whip there cannot be a good huntsman, and it is a question whether a bad whip does not do more harm than good; at all events, more than one instance occurred last season of an indifferent one completely spoiling a promised run. Jack Goddard is set down as having been almost the cleverest whip that has ridden over Leicestershire in modern times; while Machin, who was with the Quorn under Mr. Musters, and is now, I fancy, playing at fox and hounds among the flints and hops of Kent, was as good a model as could be chosen; for he never whipped hounds blindly off a scent, but put them round sharp when necessary, could ride like a bird, and was always in his proper place.

Alas! Mr. Musters' brilliant pack are no longer the Quorn. After three seasons, in which they have shewn themselves possessed of all those qualities preeminently needful for the Shires, they are now about to return to Nottinghamshire, where Mr. Musters resumes his old country. No hounds in the world could beat them to fly on a good scent, every single hound greedy to lay hold of it. Carrying it before them without one idler to take things for granted, they would spread themselves out, so that the sharpest turn seldom threw them at fault. And, with all their dash and eagerness, it was especially notable that they never allowed themselves to flash a yard over the line, or even to strike forward in hopes of picking it up again beyond the point to which they had brought it—so common a weakness of courage and excitement. Of course it has sometimes happened that they have been determinedly driven over the line by the impetuous, thoughtless crowd behind them, but often have I seen them, when running hard, spread right and left the moment they missed the guiding perfume from their nostrils, then, circling round again, take it up in front, and dash off once more with equal vigour. For actual pace in a burst, it is a question if even the Belvoir could compare with them; and yet they never forgot the lessons in steady hunting they had learnt in the colder land of Nottinghamshire. The great difficulty they had ever to fight against was the overgrown size of the Quorn fields—fields composed of every variety of element, the genuine by no means predominating on all occasions. For instance, the huge cavalcade that troops forth to join the chase whenever it is fixed for anywhere in the neighbourhood of Leicester or Loughboro', is indeed an incongruous one; though, true,

a Friday meet can also boast of such a corps of hard
and finished riders as is not to be seen at the covert-side
elsewhere. On these occasions it is next to impossible
to secure fair play for the hounds, should the scent be
a poor one, or the fox a twister. Hunting is out of the
question, and all that can be hoped for is a straight, quick
gallop, when the pack can keep moving steadily onwards.
But here we are reminded of another point which mili-
tates greatly against any certainties of sport, even in the
favoured regions we are discussing; and that is the
difficulties that beset the path of a fox, however well disposed, indeed the marvel is, that we ever find one bold
enough to face the open at all. As he crosses the big grass
fields he has no shelter from the eye of shepherd or
traveller, who can view him a mile away, and who are
only too delighted with the chance of exercising their
lungs, and proving their love of sport, by sending
screeches of fearful import after him. They are still
better pleased if they can get a sheep dog to course him,
and many a time have I heard a gentle bucolic recount
with glee how he " seed him a coming, looed on the old
dog, and uncommon nigh catched him." The sheepdogs
themselves have a natural predilection for chasing a fox;
and though, when they succeed in coming up to him he
can invariably drive them off, the run is generally ruined
by their interference. More sport is spoiled by these
pastoral scourges than any other cause; for there would
seem to be a separate dog kept for each sheep in
Leicestershire, and they are ever on the alert to do
mischief.   *   *   *   *   *
It was said only the other day by a sportsman who
numbered his years of hunting by scores, that " he had
seen one lot of riding men succeed another in Leicestershire, but he had never seen so many or so hard as those
of the present day." Lord Wilton's name will be

handed down to generations to come as the most finished rider of his day; though the past season only saw him out once, and it was even feared at one time that he would hunt no more. Lord Grey de Wilton though is never likely to let the family name lose its celebrity, for he will not be beat in the field. The fence is never too big or the pace too quick for him; he never takes his eye off the hounds when they are running, or at a momentary difficulty, and is invariably close at them; and riding vigorously at all his fences, is down but seldom. To go straight down to a rasper, without turning a yard right or left, no man that ever crossed Leicestershire can surpass Sir Frederick Johnstone; and no matter how wide the brook or strong the oxer, he will not be separated from the hounds. Nor has he only the merit of being hard, for besides being a fine horseman, he is as quick away as a rabbit; and should hounds slip suddenly off, he is almost certain to get away on the best of terms with them, though he may have been unnoticeable before. Mr. Forster, too, who so astonished the natives during his first season in these parts (the one before last, 1869—70) by the way he used to ride at big timber, still keeps up his character; and of late, has built his reputation chiefly on his talent for negotiating the almost impracticable "bottoms" with which the country abounds. *   *   *
Now we come to one who has made a wider name for himself than the world of Leicestershire has given him, and who, when well mounted, and in the full glory of a stiff country, should be seen to be appreciated, viz., Captain Smith, of steeplechase renown. *   *   *
Lord Calthorpe was going as straight as anyone last season; Colonel Forester seems to have lost neither nerve nor keenness; and Mr. Little Gilmour enjoys his hunting as much, and forms as leading and pleasant a

feature in the field as ever.   *   *   *

Mr. Banks Wright was again out with the Quorn several times this season, and gave all the younger generation a chance of picking up a wrinkle. At the top of the welters stand Mr. Fenwick and the still more heavily weighted Squire Musters, both of whom give some stone and a beating to the majority of their finer drawn companions.

The Quorn country requires little description beyond the passing allusions already made to it. No part, except perhaps a small strip round Great Dalby, is so stiff as to be impracticable; while everywhere it requires a flying hunter, and is just within the powers of a good man and a good horse to cross. It is all (mostly?) grass, with the exception of a patch of plough here and there, and when a certain amount of rain has fallen, never fails to carry a scent. The Loughborough side is very different, that along the site of the old Charnwood Forest being as little like Leicestershire as can be imagined; and though a good deal of low wet grass land lies below this rough and stony woodland country, the face of the land carries a deal of unpleasant dirt upon it. The fields, too, are a great contrast to the gay throngs that one is accustomed to see at the covert side with the crack packs. Yet Mr. Musters used to enjoy his hunting here better than on the more fashionable side, for (which is easily understood) hounds have every chance given to them.

Changing the scene, we find ourselves in High Leicestershire—a country where fox-hunting should thrive when every other part has succumbed to brick and mortar. Yet, with all its charms, it falls short of being the hunter's paradise that merely a long ride to covert would lead one to suppose. For instance, the big woods of Owston, Launde, Skeffington, Tugby and Co., may be pleasant enough for cub-hunting, but to have to bucket your horse almost to a standstill in the deep rides, and then sit down to a stern chase over the ridge and furrow and well-nigh impracticable fences of the adjoining pasturage, is not felicity to every mind. There is only one man who never is left behind, and afterwards cannot be shaken off, and that is Mr. Tailby himself. He appears to get away by a kind of instinct, and constant practice and most determined resolution enable him to make light of difficulties that choke off men twenty years his junior. It certainly is a genuine drawback to some of his best country, that the hardest field have to.tail when hounds cross it, for if negotiable at all, it is only so in one or perhaps two places; and you may lose half a field and the whole of your pleasure while waiting your turn in the crush. There are some few districts indeed which cannot be got over in a direct line at all, Skeffington lordship being about the best known.

Since the above was written, Colonel Lowther has formally signified his intention of claiming, after next season, that part of Mr. Tailby's territory which properly belongs to the Cottesmore. It will be remembered that the country which Mr. Tailby has hunted for the last fifteen years is made up of cessions (or temporary grants would express it more properly) from the Quorn and the Cottesmore, and was originally formed for Mr. Richard Sutton during his father's lifetime.

* * * Mr. Tailby's run of the season (1870—71) was just before Goodall was laid up, and was something extraordinary for distance and country. This was on Thursday, February 16th, from Shankton Holt, when they ran fast by Illston, Rolleston, and Keythorpe, over a stiff turf line to Allexton Wood, then hunted on by Manton, and at length to ground near

Lyndon, the whole distance—about a seventeen mile point—being got over in two hours and a quarter.

* * * * * *

Perhaps no country could give the same amount of pleasure to a man who keeps only about a couple of horses, likes to ride on the grass, and enjoys hunting for its own sake, as the Atherstone under its present administration. Long, slow-hunting runs are entirely Captain Thomson's forte; and, as I said before, he does what few other men ever attempt in a grass country, viz., to walk a fox to death. What a lesson, too, very many huntsmen might take from him in the matter of going to halloas, or rather *not* going to them, for he decks hunting with a beauty that one seldom sees in Leicestershire, in making his hounds work out every yard, instead of getting their heads up, and exciting them so that they never again put them properly down, and can only kill with the help of mobbing and heading. When a cold, weak scent has to be followed up, and there is no chance of your gallop, the two plans amount to a question of whether you prefer to see hounds hunting, or huntsmen and whips blowing and flogging them from field to field."

"SPORT AND WANT OF SPORT IN THE SHIRES."

TO NICOLAS,*

WHO WILL NOT ANSWER ANYTHING.

Air: "Twinkle, twinkle, little star."

Thinking, thinking vainly, ah!
How I wonder where you are!
All about the world you fly,
Like a comet in the sky,
While I'm vainly thinking, "Ah!
How I wonder where you are!"

* Nicolas Charlton, Esq., a well-known sportsman in Nottinghamshire, Yorkshire, and Leicestershire, between which countries his time is so much divided, that his friends never know where a letter will find him.

Thus in misery despondent
Sighs each wretched correspondent,
Ever writing, never getting
Answers, but for ever fretting,
While the labour and the cost
Of his letters all are lost,
And he's thinking, thinking, "Ah!
How I wonder where you are!"

If to Chilwell's frigid swamp
You despatch your postage stamp,
Nicolas you then may swear
Will be anywhere but there:
Jumping with a wild delight
On the hounds of Charley Wright,†
Or adding to his load of sins
By gammoning the trusting Binns; ‡
But, wherever he may be,
Correspondents still you see,
Thinking, vainly thinking, "Ah!
How we wonder where you are!"

16th Nov., 1884.   L. ROLLESTON.

———

MY OLD HORN:
A Song,

DEDICATED TO MY DEAR OLD FRIEND, FREDERICK
BROCKMAN, ESQ., WHO FOR THIRTY-SIX YEARS HUNTED
THE EAST KENT HOUNDS WITH UNFLAGGING
PERSEVERANCE AND SIGNAL SUCCESS.

Now up in the heather, now down in the plain,
    The secret shall never be known,
How often I've pressed it again and again,
    That sweet little lip to my own:

---

† The Badsworth.   ‡ Mr. Binns, of Leeds.

How oft on the moor to its musical note
   I've bounded away like a deer,
When far in the shade of some deep mountain glade
   Its tidings have thrilled on my ear.

One note is enough! and quickly the hounds
   O'er Dartmoor are racing away,
And for'rad they fling, like birds on the wing—
   'Tis a stout one before them to-day.
Then Echo enchanted unites with delight
   The lingering notes to prolong,
And, roused from their sleep in the cavernous deep,
   The Naiads are charmed with the song.

Together we've traversed the mountain and mere,
   By many a desolate nook,
And, strolling along, have joined in the song
   Of many a babbling brook;
Then wearied, mayhap, I've slumber'd awhile,
   Forgetting the world it would seem;
Yet still on my ear I catch a sweet cheer—
   'Tis the sound of a horn in my dream.

Other pleasures will pall, leave a poison behind,
   Or oft, like a mirage, betray;
Other lips have a snare—oh! I bid you beware,
   For I've suffered enough in my day—
But pure is that lip, and innocent, too,
   The pastime it ever promotes;
And, grey as I'm grown, I blush not to own
   That I've lavished my life on its notes.

Old friend and ally ! to bid thee 'Good bye'
   Is a struggle I long have deferred ;
Though the day is far spent, and the warning is sent,
   It chokes me to whisper the word :
But if mute thou must be, and Time's iron will
   The die of the future has cast,
In the depths of my heart thou'lt be eloquent still,
   While memory clings to the past.

Ah no, we'll not part ! As the Romans of old
   Their Larès were wont to adore,
Near my own fireside thou shalt ever preside,
   To warn away Care from my door :
There still thou shalt tell of mountain and fell,
   And many a far-away friend ;
And ever to me thy presence shall be
   A relic of joy to the end.

E. W. L. DAVIES.

A LIST OF MASTERS OF THE QUORN HOUNDS.

I SCARCELY know if it is allowable to call hounds "the Quorn" that were kept elsewhere than at Quorn, but as the hounds that hunted Leicestershire have been quartered in various kennels at different times, I shall take leave to begin my list with—

Thomas Boothby, Esq., of Tooley Park, Leicestershire, born 1677 ; died 1752.

His death is recorded in the *Gentleman's Magazine* for August, 1752, as follows : "Thomas Boothby, of Tooley Park, Leicestershire, Esquire, one of the greatest sports-

men in England." In the possession of Mr. Corbet, of
Adderley, is an old horn, partly of horn and partly of

Mr. Boothby's Horn (engraved by the kind permission of Mr. Corbet).

Ordinary Horn.

silver, with this inscription: "Thos. Boothby, Esq.,
of Tooley Park, Leicestershire.—With this horn he
hunted the first pack of foxhounds then in England
fifty-five years. Born 1677; died 1752. Now the
property of Thos. d'Avenant, Esq., county of Salop, his
grandson." This horn was engraved in the *Field* newspaper some years ago, and is, I think, one of the most
interesting mementos in England, showing that Leicestershire possessed a "crack" pack of hounds nearly 200
years ago, and that two successive sportsmen hunted the
country for more than a hundred years. In Nicholl's
History of Leicestershire I find that "Tooley Park was
purchased by Judith, Lady Corbett, and Mr. Thomas
Boothby, her son by her first husband, enjoyed it in
1648, and in that family it continued till 1779, when
Skrymshire Boothby, Esq., sold it." Mr. Thomas
Boothby, the M.F.H., married an heiress named Scrimshire or Scrymshire, and took her name in addition to his
own. He had a son, who died before him, a granddaughter,
Anne, who married, as his second wife, Mr. Meynell, and
a grandson, known as "Prince" Boothby, with whom

Mr. Meynell lived at one time, and who is often mentioned in the accounts of Mr. Meynell's sport, and as one of the first subscribers to his hounds.

"The name of Mr. Boothby is still had in reverence in the parish of Peckleton. It is even said that he was the donor of the present peal of Church Bells belonging to the place, and that he had them so pitched and tuned as to resemble the cry of a pack of hounds. Certainly the said bells are of a very melodious and cheery kind in their music. The horn to which you allude is also known by tradition in Peckleton, and the inscription on it has probably given rise to the saying, that Mr. Boothby was the first person to introduce the foxhound into England, whereas most likely it is intended to convey the idea of the great *excellence* of his pack. It is also said that Mr. Boothby altered the pattern of the hunting horn, which, until that time, was of the shape seen in old pictures slung around the body."—Letter from the REV. THE HON. AUGUSTUS BYRON.

Hugo Meynell, of Bradley, 1753 *to* 1800.—*Born* 1735; *died* 1808.

Mr. Boothby having died in 1752, the following year, 1753, Mr. Meynell, then only eighteen, began his long and successful hunting career, which ended in 1800, when, in consequence of his son's ill-health, Nicholl says, "It was thought advisable to dispose of Quorndon Hall" to Lord Sefton, who also bought the foxhounds and kennels. Mr. Meynell married first, at the age of nineteen, Miss Gell, who died in 1757; and in 1758, being then a widower of twenty-three, Miss Anne Boothby Scrimshire became his second wife. Among the many anecdotes recorded of Mr. Meynell, and the universal tribute paid to him as the great master of the modern style of foxhunting, I think no one has remarked what a debt the next generation owed to him. All over England, in the early part of this century, were masters of hounds and foxhunters who had served an apprenticeship with Meynell, and considering the extent of country over which he hunted—from Nottingham Trent Bridges to Rockingham Forest, and from the Welland to the Dove—what a vast number of boys of all ranks must have grown up in his forty-seven years of mastership to reverence the name of Meynell! Several seasons' sport enjoyed with his hounds may be found recorded in Jones' Diary, a journal kept by the whipper-in who officiated under Jack Raven, and by this one may observe, that there was no perceptible difference between the run of foxes in the last century and the present time. What strikes one most is, that the sportsmen of those days were contented to hunt less often and kill much fewer foxes than is now thought necessary. When Mr. Meynell parted with his hounds and establishment at Quorn to Lord Sefton in 1800, in consequence of his son's illness, Nicholl says, "This veteran sportsman, the oldest foxhunter in the kingdom, who has resided at Quorn for forty-seven years, has purchased a small house belonging to his huntsman, and is going to build some rooms to it, at the back of the kennels, for an occasional residence during the hunting season." The son died that same year, but Mr. Meynell lived till 1808.

Lord Sefton, 1800 *to* 1802.—*Died* 1838.

Lord Sefton has the credit of introducing second horses into the Leicestershire hunting-field; some say in consequence of *his* great weight, others, in consequence of *their* great value.

Lord Foley, 1802 *to* 1807.—*Died* 1833.

T. Assheton Smith, 1807 *to* 1817.—*Died* 1863.

The memoir, written a few years ago, is so thoroughly exhaustive, that it is not necessary to say anything about Mr. Assheton Smith's sporting career.

George Osbaldeston, 1817—1821.

The same remark applies to Mr. Osbaldeston, but I do not remember seeing it noticed in print, that when Mr. Osbaldeston hunted Nottinghamshire, he remarked that it was a most difficult country to kill foxes and (at the same time) to show sport in.

Sir Bellingham Graham, 1821 *to* 1823.—*Died* 1866.

George Osbaldeston, 1823 *to* 1827.—*Second Mastership.*

Lord Southampton, 1827 *to* 1831.—*Died* 1872.

Mr. Bernal Osborne's most amusing poem, called " Melton in 1830 : a day with Lord Southampton's hounds," refers to this period of history.

Sir Harry Goodricke, 1831 *to* 1833.—*Died* 1833.

At Sir Harry's lamented death, at the age of thirty-three, he was succeeded by his heir, *Mr. F. Holyoake,* 1833 *to* 1835.

Mr. Errington, 1835 *to* 1838.

The Sporting Magazine of 1840 says of Mr. Errington—"I once saw him stop a whole squadron of impetuous go-a-head fellows by a wave of the hand and one of those bland smiles, the magic of which has been so often said or sung." "That's more than Tom Smith or the Squire could have done, with all their bully-ragging!" said a sporting farmer. There is an extraordinary personal resemblance between Mr. Errington and Lord Chesterfield. In the poem of "The Meltonians" they are called "the Dromios of our Hunt,"—so like,

"That hang me if I know which 'tis I see,
Till smiles assure me, Errington, 'tis thee."

Lord Suffield, 1838 *to* 1839.—*Died* 1853.

Lord Suffield bought Mr. Ralph Lambton's celebrated pack of hounds for £3000, to bring to Leicestershire, but they were daunted by the crowd, and did not understand being ridden over, and consequently caused some disappointment. Lord Suffield unfortunately got into pecuniary difficulties, which resulted in the hounds and horses being seized by bailiffs, while on the way to meet at Lodge-on-the-Wolds. His lordship only hunted the Quorn country one season, and was succeeded by

Mr. Tom Hodgson, 1839 *to* 1841.—*Died* 1863.

Mr. Hodgson always hunted in a brown coat and broad-brimmed hat, which gave rise to an amusing incident, recorded in the *Sporting Magazine* of 1841. "The story runs, that when in the act of pulling down a fence near Seagrave, he was collared by a farmer, and ordered to desist. Mr. Hodgson stripped directly, and his enormous length quite astonished his antagonist, a fat, good-tempered, punchy fellow. 'Dang it, I do'ant want to fight thee, only ride over the country, and get over the fences like a man; don't make gaps one could drive a broad-wheeled wagon thro'.' The fact was, the farmer did not know Mr. Hodgson, and subsequently excused himself on the impossibility of a Leicestershire man thinking that a person in a brown coat, whom he never saw ride at a fence, could be Master of the Quorn Hounds."

Mr. Greene, 1841 to 1847.

Mr. Greene, of Rolleston, is mentioned as a prominent rider in Sir Harry Goodricke's time, and was the first Leicestershire landowner to take the hounds since Mr. Boothby. Tom Day was his huntsman, and it was during his mastership that the Quorn and Mr. Musters' hounds joined and killed their fox together near Plumtree, as described in the appendix to "Notitia Venatica."

Sir Richard Sutton, 1847 to 1856.—Died 1855.

Sir Richard had previously hunted the Burton and Cottesmore countries, in the latter of which he gave but little satisfaction, as will be seen by a letter in one of these pages, contained in Will Stansby's Diary. His kindness and hospitality, and the generous manner in which he hunted the Quorn country, caused a universal mourning there at his sudden death in the beginning of the season 1855. It must have been in 1853 or 1854 that my father took me to meet Sir Richard's hounds at Lodge-on-the-Wolds, when I was about twelve or thirteen. I remember the white collars of the men, which I was afterwards told were introduced by Sir Richard that he might the more readily distinguish his own servants in the crowd. Sir Richard first created the country now hunted by Sir Bache Cunard, by giving his son, Mr. Richard Sutton, a pack of hounds to hunt there two days a week, it being a portion of the Quorn. Mr. Banks Wright, Sir Richard's half brother, celebrated as a light weight and fine horseman, made the great reputation during his brother's various masterships, which he so justly preserved to the last years of his life.

Lord Stamford, 1856 to 1863.—Died 1883.

Mr. Clowes, 1863 to 1866.

Lord Hastings, 1866 *to* 1868.—*Died* 1868.

It was, I believe, about the last day that Lord Hastings' hounds went out, in the spring of 1868, that they had one of the best gallops seen in the Quorn country for years, finding their fox at Walton Thorns, and taking him to the Old Hills in an hour. Pike was then the huntsman.

Mr. Chaworth Musters, 1868 *to* 1870.

It was in November of Mr. Musters' first season that Lord Hastings' death occurred, and not many days afterwards Lord Somerville, who had come to Leicestershire for the season, was killed while hunting with Mr. Tailby's hounds.

The season of 1868—69 was a very good one for scent, and, consequently, for sport; and Mr. Story, of Lockington, used laughingly to say, it would be a pity if Mr. Musters could not show sport, considering that he had three huntsmen in his establishment besides himself, namely : Frank Gillard, who hunted the hounds in the high country; Bob Machin, late huntsman to the Rufford, who whipped-in to him; and John Goddard, who, after hunting the Quorn hounds and Mr. Tailby's, had undertaken the management of the stud at Quorn. Mr. Musters' health unfortunately proved unequal to the work after two seasons, and the expense greater than he could afford to continue, so he was obliged to give up the country, though most kindly pressed *to go on hunting it with* a subscription. He lent his hounds for one season, that of 1870—71, to Mr. Coupland, and they were hunted by Jem Mac-Bride; after which, Mr. Coupland bought the Craven hounds, and Mr. Musters took his own back to Nottinghamshire.

Mr. Coupland, 1870 *to* 1884.

The sport shown during Mr. Coupland's mastership is fully described in the "Cream of Leicestershire," and the name of Tom Firr will always be connected with those stirring annals of the longest enduring mastership since Meynell. On Mr. Coupland's resignation last spring, the hounds were bought by the Duke of Portland, Lord Wilton, and Mr. Behrens—Tom Firr was engaged to continue as huntsman; and eventually Lord Manners undertook the mastership, with which our record ends—the *twenty-first on the list, Lord Manners,* 1884.

L. C. MUSTERS.

THE LAST FORTNIGHT OF THE YEAR 1884.

MONDAY, DECEMBER 15TH, 1884.

RUN WITH LORD FERRERS' HOUNDS.

MET at Belton. Found in Langley New Wood, and went away through Langley Priory at a great pace, turned to the right, nearly to Lockington Gorse, left it on the left, and pointed for Belton, then over the Diseworth and Belton brooks, and, leaving Piper Wood on the left, pointed for Sheepshed. Here the fox was headed back, and they ran him between Piper and Oakley Woods, crossing the latter by the middle ride, then down the far side and away for Hathern Turn. This took about forty minutes, and was, as hounds ran, about seven miles. They then turned left along the bank of the Soar, and ran it for a mile, but crossed just opposite Mr. Paget's house. Some of the field crossed at Zouche Mill, and others at Kegworth, and the latter met the hounds just as they got over the bridge. They ran across the very middle of Kegworth Station, over both platforms and both lines of rails, and into Kingston Park, where they checked, but hit it off, and ran on across the Park, and out to the left, up to Gotham Stone Pits, and then along the hill top, and after a check there, owing to the fox lying down, they ran on over the hill and down towards Barton very fast. Here they turned to the right across the road, on over the middle of Clifton pasture, crossing the Clifton brook, which is supposed to be unjumpable, and which the field negotiated at a drinking place; straight on up to Lime Man's Rough. Here, within a field of Ruddington, some boys saw the fox close before the hounds, and they began running very hard towards Bradmore, which was left on the right, and pointing for Rancliffe Wood. Mr. Charlton here viewed the fox three fields ahead; the hounds got close to him, ran him into a little spinney between Bradmore and Plumtree, where he laid down, and, coming out in view, they raced him two fields, and ran into him on the Bradmore and Plumtree road, close to where the new railway passes Plumtree. The time was two hours and forty-four minutes. The distance, twelve miles from point to point; as the hounds ran, about twenty. Two couples were missing when the fox was killed, but they had been caught and shut up in Sutton Bonnington, where two foxes were before them, so they were not to blame. Those at the finish of this severe run were Lord Ferrers, Captain Henry, Mr. William Paget, Mr. Henry Story, Mr. Tidmas, Mr. Rolleston, Mr. Charlton, Mr. Robson, Mr. Macdonald, Mr. Brooks, Mr. Newton, Mr. Sanford, Mr. Cresswell, and Mr. Fellowes from Burton-on-Trent. One gentleman, of great hunting experience in various countries, declared this was the best run he had ever seen.

It is interesting to know that, out of the following list of hounds which worked particularly hard and well during this long run, many are descended from Mr. Musters' hounds :—

Duster, Dorimont, Dreadnought and *Destiny*, by Brocklesby Rutland, out of Dairymaid, by Belvoir Dorimont, out of Mr. Musters' Hostess.
Adelaide, by Brocklesby Alfred, out of Welfare, by Belvoir Firebrand, out of Mr. Musters' Welcome.
Bluecap and *Bracelet,* by Belvoir Brusher, out of Welcome, by Belvoir Warrior, out of Mr. Musters' Singwell.
Narrative, by Brocklesby Rutland, out of Nelly, by Belvoir Rambler, out of Mr. Francklin's Nimble.
Shiner, by Wonder, out of Scandal, by the Milton Somerset.
Necklace, by Fatal, by Mr. Musters' Forager, out of his Royalty, out of Narrative (above).

WRITTEN BY LORD FERRERS.

It was particularly satisfactory to the Editor of this book (which is dedicated to Lord Ferrers), that this great run took place just in time to be inserted in it, especially as Lord Ferrers had jokingly promised nearly a year before to run a twelve mile point on purpose.

———

RUN WITH THE DUKE OF RUTLAND'S HOUNDS.

Monday, December 22nd.—Met at Harby. Hounds had not long been in Harby Cover when a very large grey-coloured fox broke away; the pack was quickly on his line, and a regular race ensued, as straight as we

could go for Kaye Wood. Two fields short of it a
shepherd and his dog turned our fox, but this caused no
check as it generally does. Clinging to the Smite until
we crossed the canal, we then turned close to the right
of Hose Gorse, and inclined to Hose Village for a few
fields; crossed the road about midway between Hose
and Clawson, and our fox was turned by a shepherd dog
in Mr. Colman's home field; back over the road he went,
and straight for Sherbrooke's Cover, crossing the Smite
just to the right of it, after which we ran in the shape
of the letter S to Over Broughton, leaving the village
close on our left hand. Our fox's next point was in a
straight line for Willoughby; about a mile short of it,
he wheeled to the right and made for the Curate Gorse,
where we were very near to him; a man standing at the
south corner of the cover turned reynard away, and
down he went for the Midland Railway, to which he
clung, crossing and recrossing it about three or four
times, until approaching Widmerpool Station; then
leaving the iron road behind him, made for Flint Hill
plantation. We had then covered eighteen miles of
country in an hour and twenty minutes. In a minute
or so Tom Firr was seen galloping up with the Quorn
pack, and into the cover he brought his hounds, the
Belvoir being close to their fox when the Quorn joined.
Almost directly our fox was away, both packs being well
together close to his brush. A few rough ploughed
fields at the start were in favour of the fox, as scent was
rather catchy, partly owing to the number of hares on
the move. Over this little difficulty, the pace became
a smart gallop, which continued to the end. We
ran on pretty straight for Dalby, through the village,
also through Dalby Wood. We were soon going over
the railway tunnel to the left of Grimstone Gorse,
through Saxelby Spinney down to Saxelby Village,

where a turn took us to within a field of Cant's Thorns; then turned sharp down the valley to Welby Holt (or Lord Wilton's cover), where they ran for four minutes, and killed this game old fox, after one of the most exciting runs ever seen. I gave Tom Firr the head, intending to keep the brush to bring home and keep as a memento of this wonderful run; however, Mr. Coupland begged very hard for it, so I presented it to that gentleman. On measuring the distance of this fine run on the ordnance map, I find it no less than twenty-six miles, viz., from Harby Cover, by following the line hounds actually ran.

Amongst those out with us were Mr. Burdett Coutts, Mr. Lubbock, Mr. E. Chaplin, Captain Hume, Mr. Lionel Trower, M. Couturier, M. Roy, Mr. C. A. Brown, Mr. Fisher, Dr. Williams, Master Knowles, Mr. Henry Smith, Junior, Mr. Marriott, &c.

F. GILLARD.

(The point from Harby Cover to Widmerpool is seven miles; from Widmerpool to Welby Holt also seven, as the crow flies.)

Gillard says, in a letter he wrote me soon afterwards, "I noticed one of the Quorn hounds making a good hit on two occasions, and on making enquiries how she was bred, was told she was a daughter of Belvoir Weathergage. It certainly was by far the finest run I ever saw, and I think a better line of country could not be picked in Leicestershire. The first twenty minutes over the vale would no doubt be put down as the best part of this run by those who are fond of a fast thing. Hounds raced from Harby Cover to Clawson, after which we were kept galloping along at a smartish pace. Never getting sight of my second horse, my old 'Gameboy,' true to his name, carried me from beginning to end, and he missed but very few fields which the pack crossed all throughout."

TUESDAY, DECEMBER 23RD, 1884.

RUN WITH MR. JARVIS'S HOUNDS.

WE met at Langford Hall.—A beautiful morning, and very still. What wind there was, north-west. Drew the two little covers by Langford Hall and Winthorpe Car covers blank. Found our fox in the cover adjoining Coddington Hall, which I drew by permission of Major Tempest, acting master of the Blankney Hounds.

Ran down the Park, and crossed the Newark and Sleaford turnpike at the bottom of the hill, where he was coursed by a sheep dog across the first field. He ran within one field of the Great Northern Railway, and turned back to the left through Coddington Plantations by Barnby Manor, which he left just to his left hand, crossed the river Witham just below Beckingham Village—we luckily found a bridge about two hundred yards from where the hounds crossed. They ran on, leaving Fenton to the left, to within three fields of Stubton, where we checked. Hit the line off again to the right, leaving Claypole Station on the left, by the side of the railway, to close opposite Balderton Manor House, when he crossed the line, the last hound just getting over before the Express came by. They ran through the little plantations at Balderton, and crossed the Great North Road at their southernmost end, apparently pointing for Cotham Thorns; here we had a very long check. I held them

on over a large ploughed field, and luckily they hit it off
on the grass beyond, and he then crossed the Newark
and Melton Railway at Hawton brickyard, where he
was viewed five minutes before us, the only time he was
seen since leaving Coddington. He went straight down
to the river Devan, and crossed it into a willow osier.
We found a bridge in the next field but one, Harry
Brown, my whip, wading through the river to get on
to Mr. Brockton's horse, which he kindly offered him
to save time. We then left Thorpe Village to the left,
on to the big grass field outside the Park at Stoke, where
we crossed the Foss Road. He turned to his right into
Stoke Holt, and ran alongside the river Trent, which I
thought for a moment he meant to cross. My second
horseman, however, hallooed him away from Stoke Holt
and he ran back by Thorpe, crossing the line we had
come, and by Elston, where he turned to his right, and
again crossing the Foss Road, we ran into him, within
two fields of Mr. Fillingham's house at Syerston. Those
who saw this run to the end were Mr. Wray, of Thurlby
Hall, Mr. Cecil Smith Woolley, of Collingham, Mr.
Aitcheson, of Thurlby, Mr. N. Cockburn, of Lincoln,
Mr. Baily, of Collingham, Mr. Brockton, of Farndon,
brother of the celebrated steeplechase rider, and two
others, besides myself and Harry Brown. George Marshall, my second horseman, came up with us at Stoke.
The time was two hours and forty minutes. The farthest
point was nine miles and a half, in the course of which
we crossed three rivers and two railways, and ran out
of the Blankney through the Belvoir into the South
Notts. country.

G. E. JARVIS.

RUN WITH LORD GALWAY'S HOUNDS.

FRIDAY, DECEMBER 26th.

THESE hounds had one of the most remarkable runs on Friday within the memory of living sportsmen. Being Christmas time the houses of the country gentry are full of company, and a large field, including many strangers, turned up at the meet, which was at Gringley-on-the-Hill. With Viscount and Viscountess Galway, M.P., from Serlby Hall, were her ladyship's sister and Mr. Gosling; from Osberton, Mr. F. J. S. Foljambe, M.P., and Mr. Godfrey Foljambe; from Sheffield, Mr. Wilson Mappin, Mr. Firth, and Mr. Vickers; Mr. H. Beevor, Barnby Moor; Mr. Strathfield, of Rossington; Miss Ellison, Mr. C. Thorold, Mr. S. and Mr. J. White, of Leverton; Mr. E. and Mr. W. Smith, Gringley; Mr. C. Wright, Auston; Dr. Dawson, Mr. F. Raynes, Bawtry; Mr. Orlando Bridgeman Simpson, Mr. C. Marshall, and Mr. A. White, Retford; Mr. G. Bingley, Mr. and Mrs. Otter, Eaton Hall; and many others. A first move was made to Gringley Gorse, where Morgan at once hallooed a fox away, which did not stay to be found—and a rare game one he proved to be. With the large field streaming after him he pointed for Walkeringham, but after going over three fields he turned to the right, leaving Pear Tree-hill just on the left, and over the Gainsborough Road skirting Clayworth Wood, and nearly up to Wheatley Grange. The pace and the heavy country had already begun to tell upon some of the field, when he turned to the left, and took his pursuers on to Bole Fields and over the Gainsborough Road to the left of

Wheatley Village, and away at a good hunting pace over West Burton Farm to Sturton-en-le-Steeple, turning to the left and over the Manchester, Sheffield, and Lincolnshire Railway to the village, which he threaded, and away on the west side nearly to North Leverton; but here he turned over the Leverton Road and on to Fenton Bank, straight away to the gorse, through it, and on to Littleborough, threading the small osier bed, and running parallel with the Trent up to Cottam Osiers, down to the railway bridge over the Trent and Torksey, and away still at a racing pace to the earths at Rampton, which he found stopped against him, and rattled on without lingering to Fleet Plantation, and skirting it away to Colonel Eyre's osiers on the Trent bank, but turned short to the left, went back with those of the numerous field who had managed to survive by Torksey Bridge, recrossing the railway, and running nearly the same line back to Littleborough, the hounds literally racing with their fox for a hundred yards in front up to Fenton Gorse, and nearly up to Sturton, where he turned sharp round into Fenton Bank, and here they ran up to him, but he still tried hard to beat them, and the brook gave him a short respite. But they were not to be denied and pulled him down in Mr. Cobb's garden, after a grand hunting run of two hours and twenty-five minutes, which will not be forgotten by those who were up at the finish.

LETTER FROM MR. RAYNES, OF BAWTRY, AGED 84, TO THE EDITOR.

Dear Mrs. Musters,
    Any details I can give of the great run up to Sturton must of necessity be only second-hand, as my riding in

such a run is out of all question. From what I hear from those in it, the description in the paper is faithful and reliable. At Sturton it became intermittent, with frequent casts, some very wide, in which the Viscount shewed great knowledge, patience, and perseverance. The last cast to Cottam Osiers was a very long one, and I thought a forlorn one; but "Hope springs eternal," &c., and it answered. There were the two chances, the run fox and a fresh one: fortune favoured the brave, and Morgan assured me the killed fox was the Gringley fox. It was indeed a remarkable run, but nothing to stop a hunting man, or tire a horse in good condition. The country was not heavy, as described in the paper, for I never saw the clays ride better, in which I am borne out by Beevor and many others. My little nag witnessed the obsequies, and trotted home as lively as a kitten. I enclose the account of the run from the Retford paper, and of the following Monday's proceedings.

I should say, knowing the country, and accepting the description as reliable, it was a far better day's sport than the Gringley day, but perhaps not so satisfactory to the Viscount, killing his fox after two hours and twenty-five minutes, under great difficulties, in which he delights. The Monday's sport would be the best for the riding man. Lord Galway can do and appreciate both. * * * * *

Yours very truly,
F. RAYNES.

RUN WITH THE SOUTH NOTTS. HOUNDS.

On Tuesday, December 23rd, these hounds met at Pinxton Station, and trotted off to Alfreton Park for their first draw, with, however, no result; and then Lord Harrington drew Shaw Wood, the Wingfield Coverts, and Linway Springs, none of which, however, held a fox. He then went on to Ogston Carr, drawing Clattercotes on the way blank, but in the Carr, one of the right sort was soon afoot, and in a few minutes a fine old fox broke at the lower end. Hounds were out directly after him, and drove him along at a good pace, bending to the right underneath the hill opposite Overton, but before reaching the latter place, he turned to the left, and went straight up the hill side to the top of High Ordish. Here the pace, which had up to this point been very fast, still further increased, and hounds raced on over Critchlow Farm on to Tansley Common, turning again to the right past the reservoir, and out on to the open moor. They now went straight to Sydnop without a check at all—too fast for horses to keep up with them—but, on reaching the last-named place, some slow hunting ensued, until about a mile further on hounds came to a check in a plantation by Flash Dam. Up to this point they had run about ten miles. After about half an hour's delay here, they hit off either the same line or another, and ran a fair pace back to the Chesterfield and Matlock road, which they crossed about a mile above the " Lord Nelson " Inn, and from here getting on better terms with their fox, they ran fast right back to Ogston Carr, where they originally found. From the Carr back again took two hours and a half,